A Precious Window of Time
A manual for teaching & nurturing middle school girls

Copyright © 2008 by Howard Hanger
A Lobster Press Book

All rights reserved. No part of this book may be reproduced by any mechanical, photographic, or electronic process, or in the form of a photographic recording, nor may it be stored in a retrieval system, transmitted or otherwise copied for public or private use without the written permission of the publisher. Requests for permission should be addressed to:

Lobster Press
Hanger Hall
31 Park Avenue North
Asheville, NC 28801

1st Printing, November 2008
Book Design: Darlene Moore, www.moorecreativity.biz
Proofreading: Windsor Hanger, Sarah Patton
Manufactured in the United States of America

ISBN: 978-0-615-25435-7

A PRECIOUS WINDOW
of TIME

A manual for teaching & nurturing middle school girls

By Howard Hanger & Dr. Vicki Garlock

*We dedicate this book to our daughters
and to all daughters everywhere
that they might keep alive the joy of learning
and the delight of being precisely who they are.*
- Howard & Vicki

TABLE OF CONTENTS

HOWARD'S INTRODUCTION
VICKI'S INTRODUCTION
1) CRUCIAL COMMUNITY 1
    It's About Connections
    A Sense of Coming Home
    So Many Communities, So Little Time
    Not Time Sensitive
    Uniforms and Community
    Teachers Need Community Too
    And Parents...
    Community Will Be Found
    Creating Community
    The Circle Dance – Ancient Wisdom

2) STRUCTURE & FLEXIBILITY 18
    Chaos and Order
    The Chaos and Order Dance
    Bones and Muscle
    Awkwardness and Self-Consciousness
    Rules for School and Home
    Spontaneity and Flexibility
    Clarity and Consistency
    Changing the Rules
    Care and Compassion
    It's All About Balance

3) THINKING ABOUT THINKING 32
    Stage Theory and Piaget
    Sensorimotor Stage: 0-2 Years
    Preoperational Stage: 2-7 Years
    Concrete Operations Style 7-11 Years
    Formal Operations: Puberty through Adulthood
    Formal Operations: Reasoning Abstractly
    Formal Operations: Reflecting on Multiple Perspectives
    Formal Operations: Systematic Problem Solving
    Rethinking Ages and Stages

4) PURPOSE, GOALS & REFLECTION 46
What's the Goal of of Education?
Setting Life Goals
Compasses and Landmarks
Utilizing the Gift of Your Years
Working it Out
PAG's & PLG's
Making the World a Better Place
Constancy and Consistency
Reflection: Making it Real – Helping it Stick

5) THE SOCIAL SCENE 62
Who Am I?
Erikson and Personality Development
Industry and Inferiority
Identity and Role Confusion
A Brief History of Self-Esteem
Where are we now?
Self Consciousness and Emotionality
Pin the Tail on the Culprit
Ch…Ch…Ch…Changes

6) DEALING WITH FEELINGS 76
Blame It On The Amygdala
One Brain – Three Parts
Here Come The Hormones
OK, It's Not All Amygdala's Fault
Feelings… Whoa, Whoa, Whoa, Feelings
What Works?
The Guidelines: Ask & Listen
Remember: You Have Feelings, Too

7) SOCIAL SKILLS 94
Socialization Happens
You Are a Role Model. Always.
Social Skills Don't Just Happen
Connections and Boundaries

    The Top Ten Social Skills (A Starter List)
    Keeping the Main Thing The Main Thing

8) MOVING FORWARD (THEORETICALLY SPEAKING) 110
    What Makes a Good Theory?
    Spiritual Development
    Fowler's Stages of Faith
    Intuitive Projective Stage
    Mythic-Literal Stage
    Synthetic-Conventional Stage
    Beyond Synthetic-Conventional
    Alternative Theoretical Approaches
    Information Processing Approach
    Vygotsky: In the Zone

9) EXPLORATION 126
    The Nature of the Age
    Exponential Learning and Thinking
    Exploring Social Connections
    Exploring the Abstract
    Exploring with a variety of Stimuli
    Exploring the Social Connections
    The Dreaded Sexual Exploration
    Exploration with Friends
    Loners
    Exploration with Adults
    Exploring Physically
    Eating Disorders
    Transforming Travel
    Learning to Live Outside the Comfort Zone & Deal With the Unexpected
    Four East Pieces
    Allowing Her to (Sometimes) Lead the Way

10) ACADEMICS 148
    The Creative Mix
    The Basics
    Active Learning
    Reflective Learning

Raising the bar
What Does It Mean To Be Smart?
The Study of Living Life in its Fullest

POSTSCRIPT

INTRODUCTION: HOWARD HANGER

I'm a Dad. For me, that's where this book begins and ends. I'm the father of two daughters. Make that, two amazing daughters. My daughters have never stopped astounding and confounding me. They are the lights of my life.

But then, all children are amazing. Each and every one is astounding and confounding. I have long proposed a bumper sticker that reads: If you're a parent and not amazed, you're not paying attention!

Birth to young adulthood (the latter, admittedly being a moving target) is one of the most dynamic and fast-changing periods of human life. Physical, emotional, social and mental buds are blossoming moment by moment. They come into flower faster than you can ever record or even notice. Some of these blossoms will bear fruit; some will wilt and die. But watching a child develop is akin to watching a high-speed video of a fruit tree or vegetable plant in which months of growth and development are compressed to 2-3 minutes. If you are truly paying attention to a child's development, you will see changes on a daily basis every day. Every bloomin' day!

This book focuses on 3-4 of the most crucial developmental years in a child's life. It is these years, which, in many ways, determine the self-confidence, quality of life and overall happiness of the emerging adult for the next 60-80 years. Some call these 3-4 years, "puberty," some, "early adolescence." Some call it, "a pain in the butt." But, whatever you call it, it is arguably, the most crucial time in a human life to develop a sense of self: a sense of who you are, how you relate to the world around you and how you will operate in the world the rest of your days.

Mary Pipher and the AAUW

In 1994, my daughters were 6 and 8 years old, respectively. That year, Mary Pipher published a book called, Reviving Ophelia. Also in the early '90's, the American Association of University Women (AAUW) published a paper called, "What's Smart for Girls." Both of these pieces focused on girls - on the enormous struggles and incredible possibilities for girls during the pubescent years. As the father of two future pubescent girls, both of these pieces got my attention.

Ophelia is a character in Shakespeare's "Hamlet." As a young girl, Ophelia is happy and free; but during adolescence, she loses herself; and when she falls in love with Hamlet, she begins living only for his approval and for the approval of her father. She loses her sense of inner direction and when Hamlet spurns her, she goes mad with grief and drowns in elegant clothes that weigh her down and pull her under.

Mary Pipher uses this image ever-so-effectively in painting the picture of what all-too-often happens to adolescent girls today: Living only for the approval of boys or of peers and trying desperately to look like/act like/think like/be like the girls in the magazines… the girls on TV and the movies… the rock-star/movie-star/airbrushed/flowing-haired/perfectly-clothed-or-unclothed-wrinkle-fat-and-blemish-free media models who are constantly and consistently exalted by our culture with fame and rewarded with big bucks, as the representation of what a women should be.

And what happens in so many cases, I have discovered, is that our young girls – in trying to accomplish the impossible task of emulating these media models – lose themselves. They forget who they are. And, in attempting to "be" something they can never be, they drown in cultural sea of unattainable body image and fashion expectations.

The Beginning of Hanger Hall School
So it was, that the influence of Mary Pipher's book and the report by the AAUW, led me to start a middle school for girls. Admittedly, it was a selfish act. I wanted this for my daughters; and finding that there was nothing like this in my neck of

the woods, I started interviewing educators across the country, borrowed some money, hired a teacher and, in 1999, opened the doors in our home as Hanger Hall – A School for Girls. My original intent was to get my daughters through the school and then, either close it or let someone else operate it. There were only three students during the first year, one of them, my oldest daughter.

At Hanger Hall School, we set up founding principles to which we still adhere:
• We agreed to follow much of the model set up in AAUW's "What's Smart for Girls," which emphasized the need for many single-gender experiences and small classrooms.
• We established as our motto: Nurturing the girl and empowering the emerging woman.
• We agreed that our curriculum would be focused on two equally weighted premises: academic growth and personal growth.
• We implemented a program called "What It Means to Be a Woman in the 21st Century," in which we bring in a different woman each week - women with varying lifestyles, careers, ages, body shapes, sexual orientations, ethnicities and religions who speak and answer the girls' questions on what it means to be a woman.
• We put into action a travel program for the girls, taking them out of their comfort zone and into the world, as a tried and true means of self-discovery.
• We established regular meetings of what we call "Group," during which current school issues (pleasant or painful) are discussed; and interpersonal conflict resolution is taught, expressed and encouraged.

Throughout this book, you will find references to Hanger Hall School. It is this School which has become the proving ground for the effectiveness of single-gender, self-awareness education and nurture.

Sex, the Tip of Iceberg. The Big Question, "Who Am I?"
So often in our culture, when the topic of middle school and middle-schoolers comes up in conversation, one of the first words you hear is "hormones." And yes,

this is when the sexual organs and glands kick into high gear. Yes, this is when hair pops out in adult places, bodies change shape and hormones rocket themselves into every cell from sole to solar plexus to scapula to scalp. This is when mama's little baby becomes capable of making a baby herself. And that's huge! But, more and more parents and educators have come to realize that as important as sexual development may be, it's not the whole story. All too often in the past, it has been only the sexual development of this age on which parents and schools have focused.

In the past, we have given our middle-school children books and videos on sex. We have done our best to have open discussions with them. We have talked about condoms and STD's and tampons and bras and pregnancy and deodorants and reputations. We have talked about wet dreams and menstruation and breast size and erections and pimples and (sometimes, if we were brave) masturbation. And, if and when we got to the point where we thought our children "knew" enough about sex, we assumed that we had done our job. We had taught them well. "We have dealt with the pubescent issue," we would proudly say. "Thank God we're done with Sex-Ed." And we breathed a sigh of relief and went back to helping them with math, spelling, astronomy and cleaning up their bedrooms.

The point our educational systems has so often missed is this: It's one thing to know how reproduction works - how babies are made. It's yet another to know who you are and to have a sense of your self. And then, with that self-awareness, to assimilate your incredible creative sexual power, your inconceivably colossal urge and to come to grips with what you do with it on a daily basis. Without a sense of who you are, sex becomes a time-bomb waiting to happen. Sex becomes a life-long potential problem rather than a pleasure-and-life-giving blessing.

And that may well be why nature chooses this time – this sexually-charged and charging time – to offer these elder children - these emerging adults - the chance to discover themselves - to discover who they are as individuals... to realize their own one-of-a-kind way of living and dealing with the world.

This is the time of life when brain and body are given a phenomenal opportunity to develop a self-concept, a sense of individuality, an awareness of gift and talent, strength and potential which no one else in the world can ever clone. It is that oh-so-essential recognition of WHO I AM AS A PERSON (not just a reproductive being) which offers the tools to deal with whatever may come - from the inside or outside - from sexual urges to social pressure - from worries and doubts to rejection and failure - from excitement and joy to parties and celebration. We now know how momentously vital this process is; and many educators and parents today are actively exploring ways to facilitate and encourage this incredibly vital pubescent process of self-discovery.

So What Works with Girls?
This is a book about two things: 1) what needs to be happening on a developmental level with girls of this age, and 2) what works with middle school girls to allow these developmental processes to happen in a healthy way. This is a book detailing both what is needed and what actually works in helping young girls move into young womanhood.

What you will find here is not simply theory. The "how-to" chapters are based on actual experience at Hanger Hall School and at other single gender schools in the U.S. These chapters offer specific details and suggestions of how parents and educators can provide the soil, water and nutriment for a girl to grow into the utterly unique adult she is made to be.

Each of the chapters has within it with an underlying theory: that, in order to effectively assist a young girl to move into womanhood with a dynamic and growing self-awareness, we must understand that this is a process. It doesn't happen all at once. Nor, does it happen the same way with every individual.

If, as parents, coaches, group leaders and educators, we are to truly offer a guiding hand in this vital progression into self-discovery, we must work with the individual mind and body, knowing that each girl is unique. We must work with the natural development process - the mind and body's natural timetable. And, that timetable for developing self awareness is clearly sometime during the middle school years - somewhere between the ages of 10-14.

Middle school girls are not little adults. Nor are they big kids. They are amazing individuals in an incredibly unique phase of life - a stage in their time on this earth which can never, ever be repeated. These are the magical years. The irreplaceable years. These years are, indeed, a most precious window of time.

INTRODUCTION: VICKI GARLOCK

I'm a psychologist. Most people assume that I must be a therapist or a clinician of some sort – that I analyze people. In truth, I've never even taken a course about abnormal psychology or counseling. I'm a research psychologist. I think my jargon-laden designation would be a "cognitive developmental neuroscientist." As a graduate student I studied rat brains for a while – the serotonin system of the cerebellum to be more exact. Then I switched to cognitive development in children. My dissertation focused on language-related predictors of reading achievement in 4- to 8-year-olds. I found academically interesting results, and my dissertation was published in a respectable journal. If you slogged through it, the reading achievement measures would probably make sense to you. The "psycholinguistic" measures and the overall conclusions probably would not. Such is the nature of doctoral dissertations.

I then worked for 11 years as a professor at Warren Wilson College, a small liberal arts institution near Asheville, North Carolina. I taught all sorts of courses, including Biopsychology, Drugs and Behavior, Learning and Conditioning, and Cognition. But one of my primary responsibilities was teaching Infant and Child Development. My developmental courses were fairly typical in the content covered, and nearly all developmental textbooks spend at least one chapter on theories. My courses were also typical in that they drew students from several different majors. At Warren Wilson, those majors included Psychology, Education, and Outdoor Leadership. There were always a few soon-to-be young parents thrown into the mix as well.

Their youthful energy constantly pushed me to devise more clever and creative ways to make class sessions come alive. But this particular combination of students also forced me, year after year, to figure out how the theories could be applied in real life. The Outdoor Leadership students wanted the theories applied to ropes courses and group initiatives. The Education majors wanted the theories applied to classroom dynamics and behavioral management techniques. The Psychology majors wanted to know how they could better help at-risk kids. And the parents just wanted to know what in the heck any of it had to do with raising a baby!

The entire enterprise prompted me to rethink what those pesky theories truly had to offer in the first place. Why did I enjoy teaching them so much? Were they really important enough for the students to learn? And what value did they hold in my own life? It's possible that earning a Ph.D. heightened my skills of rationalization and justification. After all, I spent eight years in graduate school earning not much more that minimum wage. Surely it was worth something! Regardless of the motivation, I think there are at least three major ways in which psychological theories are useful.

Partitioning Development

Development is not just amazing; it's also complex. Psychologists have addressed this problem by dividing development up into three broad categories – 1) physical development, 2) cognitive development, and 3) social/emotional development. Physical development refers to motor milestones, such as crawling, walking, running, and throwing. It can also refer to biochemical issues, like genetic tendencies, hormone increases during puberty, and chemical imbalances that underlie mental illness. The physiology of the brain is also included in this category.

Cognitive development refers to those aspects of development that relate to thinking, memory, attention, and learning. Language development is usually placed in this category. The study of intelligence and the creation of intelligence measures are included as well.

Social/emotional development encompasses relationships with others (including family members, peers, and teachers), acquiring an understanding of culturally-appropriate emotional displays and developing a sense of self. Gender development and the role of self-esteem are also good examples of research topics that fall under this heading.

The categories are clearly arbitrary. The lines between them are also extremely blurry. Take piano lessons as an example. Clearly, the act of striking the keys in a particular order is physical. The hands and fingers should be held in a particular position, and a coordinated sequence of muscle movements must be executed. However, piano lessons are also cognitive. Players learn the piece by practicing, they think about the intentions of the composer, and they pay attention to particular details such as tempo and loudness. Piano lessons are also social/emotional. Pupils have a relationship with their teachers, there are emotions to be understood and conveyed through the music, and the act of performing can be an emotional experience.

The same is true of developmental theorists. Piaget's theory is almost entirely cognitive, but his insight into how the mind works yields wonderful clues about the expanding social world of middle school girls. Fowler, who developed a comprehensive theory of spiritual development, represents a blend of both cognitive theory and social theory. And nearly all theorists acknowledge the importance of physical maturation, particularly brain development.

In the end, however, the three categories – physical, cognitive, and social/emotional – allow us to parse complex, real-world scenarios. They allow researchers to focus on certain aspects of a situation, and they provide a potentially useful framework for understanding multifaceted events. The trick is to avoid getting boxed in and constrained by them.

Outlining Trends

Psychological theories also summarize frequently observed trends. Researchers will probably always argue about the precise relationship between nature and nurture. There will probably always be a tension between individual differences and group tendencies. And even a mediocre anthropologist will tell you that you can't ignore, side-step, or eliminate cultural effects. But certain aspects of development look eerily similar across time and place.

Take language learning as an example. No two children learn language in exactly the same way. Some children focus on individual sounds; other children focus on the overall tone. Some children speak early and often; other children remain largely silent until they utter nearly complete sentences. The order in which specific words are learned depends on what a child finds interesting, what parents choose to teach and what the culture finds important. Nevertheless, nearly all children utter their first words – even if they don't sound exactly like adult-like words – around the age of 1 year. Some time around age 2, toddlers acquire about 10 words a day, including the ones you were hoping they didn't hear. Next, they form 2-3 word "sentences." And the words in those sentences usually follow the basic grammatical rules of the native language. These trends are observed across all sorts of children who live in a variety of linguistic circumstances. If your child deviates slightly from the expected curve, there's little reason to worry. But if your three-year-old has not yet uttered a rudimentary word-like sound, someone ought to be paying attention to that.

Piaget (See Chapter 3) and Erikson (Chapter 5) were both keen observers of the human condition. They were literally masters at noticing and outlining developmental trends. Of course, not everyone agrees with their conclusions. Their theories have been tweaked, revised, criticized, and haled. But rarely are they totally ignored. My husband often says, "It's good to have a family schedule. That way, we all know what we're deviating from." As you will see, there have been some flat-out alternatives to the theories of Piaget and Erikson (Chapter 8). And those alternative theories now have their own proponents and detractors. But, more often than not, the theories of Piaget and Erikson operate like the family schedule. They serve as the foundation for modern-day psychological thought. Researchers can extend certain concepts, adjust age ranges, and identify sub-stages, but at least everyone knows what trends they're deviating from.

Supplying Terminology

Any college student in an introductory survey course can tell you that a lot of time is spent learning new terms. Open up a psychology textbook sometime and look at all the words printed in bold. Those highlighted terms are usually the vocabulary words associated with the discipline. Textbook authors love to put those words, along with their definitions, in boxes down the margins of the page. Students love to ignore them. After all, they assume those boxes exist simply to make the book look more colorful. Both groups have a point.

The problem with all these terms is that they're often just complicated labels for age-old happenings. But that's precisely why they're powerful. Take Pavlov and his dogs as an example. Ivan Pavlov was a Russian physiologist who studied the digestive system, including the salivary glands. He noticed that the dogs often began salivating when they heard the footsteps of the research assistant. He eventually coined the terms unconditional stimulus, unconditional response, conditional stimulus, and conditional response to describe the food, the footsteps, and the salivation behavior. But, Pavlov did not teach dogs to salivate to food. Or to salivate to the promise of food as predicted by footsteps. Presumably, dogs have been behaving that way since the dawn of dog time. So why is Pavlov so famous? He's famous, in part, because he systematically analyzed a phenomenon that no one had studied before. He then defined his findings – in somewhat complicated terms that we "strongly encourage" undergraduates to learn. The terms are new; the behaviors they describe are not.

When I was pregnant, I was often asked – by students and faculty alike – if I thought my educational training would make me a better parent or a more annoying parent. My kids might argue that I'm not the best person to answer that question, but I am quite certain of at least one thing: as a parent, I use my background in psychological theory every single day. Of course, you don't need a Ph.D. or a background in psychology to enjoy parenting. Development is inherently fascinating and exciting. But parenting can be frustrating and exhausting, and I find the theories comforting. I try not to foist my intellectual lingo on my husband too often, but I like being able to name what I'm seeing when I see it. And I like being able to articulate my observations – even if it's just to myself.

Precious Window

My father told me in 6th grade that I should be a professor when I grew up. I had cheerleading try-outs that day after school, and I thought his comment was just about the dumbest idea I had heard all morning. I'm sure I rolled my eyes. I realize now that his unbending belief in my worth was sure to result in something powerful. Of course, it wasn't just my dad. My mom, my grandparents, my teachers, and my coaches were all wonderful influences – at least most of them were, most of the time.

Given my psychological background, I now find it interesting that this conversation with my dad is one of my more prominent middle school memories. The idea that I would "become something" at some future point in time was just beginning to register with me; the notion that there might be a profession that was somehow a match for my personality and skills was still beyond my grasp. But my dad knew. He knew that I was poised to leave childhood behind. He knew that soon I would be driving the car and applying to college. He knew that I was on the verge of exploring all of life's possibilities – either in actuality or in my imagination. And my dad was planning ahead. He wanted to throw his suggestion out there on the front end. As it turns out, it was more than a decade before I, too, decided that I should be a professor. Lucky for me, my dad knew enough to take advantage of our precious window of time. Hopefully, this book will allow you to take advantage of yours.

- One -
CRUCIAL COMMUNITY

Hanger Hall is just like a big family. You just feel at home here. - Patricia, grade 7

It's All About Connections

Middle-school girls love connections - all kinds of connections. They like to feel connected to friends, to clubs, to athletic organizations, to church or civic groups and especially to other girls. They want to feel connected to their culture as well - to whatever is considered "hot" or current by their peers or by the culture at large. Some want to check out fashion magazines. Some never want to miss certain TV shows. Some simply "have to" see whatever movie is considered "really cool" by their friends.

Like any human at any age, middle school girls want to feel accepted, loved and respected by their peers, their parents and any other important persons in their lives. But, girls this age want more than acceptance. They want to feel a vibrant connection. They want to feel as if they are actually part of what's happening. They want to be an expression of whatever in their culture is considered the way to be.

The way to look. The way to act. Middle-school girls are always seeking some community or communities to be part of - communities with which to be connected. The community might be a soccer team or a dance class. It could be a school band or a gymnastics group. Or it could be a gaggle of friends who get together on an irregular basis for movies, pizza or sleep-overs.

A Sense of Coming Home

It is important to remember that all groups are not necessarily communities. Simply because a girl shows up regularly for her swim-team practice, does not at all mean that she has found community. A community is far more than several people getting together for whatever reason. Good community requires:

1) regular get-togethers of the same or mostly-the-same people;
2) a common goal, purpose or interest;
3) sharing, interaction, exchange of ideas and feelings, companionship;
4) a sense of deep connection-with and support-from others in the community.

Middle-school girls work best and feel more comfortable in small groups. Particularly, small groups of all girls. Make that, all middle school girls. Single gender schools have a huge advantage in that regard when it comes to the creation of community. When the class Middle-school girls work best and feel more comfortable in small groups. Particularly, small groups of all girls. Make that, all middle school girls. Single gender schools have a huge advantage in that regard when it comes to the creation of community.

Go to any middle-school social event and you will see these facts borne out before your very eyes. At a middle-school dance, for example, the girls tend to cluster in small groups with other girls. The boys cluster with other boys. Each group may be talking about the other, of course; but very little interaction is going on. Brief forays happen here and there between one gender cluster and another. But, by and large, each of the gender pods keep to themselves.

Many, if not most 11-12 year-old boys, actually display precious little interest in relating in any way - at any time - to any girl his own age. The 11-12 year-old girls, on the other hand, might be more interested in the boys than vice-versa; but they would far rather talk and giggle amongst themselves than actually attempt a conversation with the object of their own girl-to-girl conversations. Girls of middle school age like to be with girls of middle school age. Period.

So Many Communities, So Little Time

The beauty of providing community and/or making community available for our middle school girls, is that there are so many options: soccer teams, basketball teams, swim teams, concert and marching bands, dance, art and gymnastic classes. There are church groups, hiking and equestrian clubs, girl scouts, track and cross-country programs. Not all of these may be single gender organizations; but, if you look around, you discover that there are many, many single gender options out there. It's as if our culture actually knows something of what's needed.

And, if there's nothing apparent that appeals to your daughter or student, then you, as teacher or parent, can help her find others who share her interests. Nor does it have to be a formally stated interest. Lots of middle school girls love to simply listen to music and yak about whatever feels important or fun at the time. A weekly pizza party with friends can be the foundation of community. Sleep-overs (which might be more accurately called "very-little-sleep overs") are wonderful ways for middle-school girls to kindle, develop and expand friendships - friendships which can become community.

There's an old adage that says, "Home is where – when no one else wants you – they have to take you in." That's what community is all about. When you are part of a community and you get together with that community, it feels like you have come home - home, where you are loved and wanted, home, where you are known and appreciated, home, where you feel deeply connected to others with your body, heart, mind, and yes… especially your soul.

School can provide community; but schools have to work at it. One of the problems with most public and many independent schools is the sheer size in numbers. It's difficult to find community in a school of 600 – 800 + students or even in a classroom of 25-30. Likewise, when a teacher is under pressure to cover a certain amount of material or prepare the students for a required standardized test (the results of which often determine the teacher's standing, salary and even employment), there is very little time or interest left for community-building activities. Not to mention dealing with apathy, bullying, belligerence, violence, antagonism, hormonal meltdowns and the daily host of administrative interruptions with which every teacher must somehow deal.

Middle school girls love to be with each other: to do each others' hair, practice doing make-up on each other, play dress-up, sing or dance together. Unlike middle-school boys, girls this age are very comfortable with touching each other's bodies, holding hands, playfully piling up on top of each other, sleeping together side-by-side. Nor is this so much a sexual thing as it is a way of being connected.

In the country of Turkey, it is very common for heterosexual men to walk together arm-in-arm, or to kiss each other on the cheek as a greeting or farewell. Now, to the average U.S. citizen, these common intimacies seem utterly out of place, because as a culture, the men of Turkey can appear to be extremely macho and patriarchal. In Turkey's traditional family structure, it is the men who "wear the pants." So, to watch these macho men walk down the street arm-in-arm and kiss each other in greeting and farewell can be entirely confusing.

Likewise, with middle-school girls: whereas boys their age would never physically touch each other except with a pat on the back or maybe a handshake, would never sit on each others' lap or mess with the other's hair, these girls of the same age – coming from the same traditions and culture as the boys – don't even think twice about it. Girl-to-girl physical intimacy comes as naturally as girl-to-girl giggles. And it has nothing to do with homosexuality or heterosexuality. It has everything to do with the desire for connection.

Now, it interesting to note that boys do touch each other in their sports. Middle school boys are big on contact sports: football, ice hockey, rugby, wrestling, judo, karate, kick-boxing. Girls this age tend to lean more toward the sports with less contact: soccer, track, basketball, softball, gymnastics, horse-back riding. So, both genders do find ways to have contact with others their age - actual physical contact. But it's definitely different venues and means of contact for boys and girls.

Whether it's an organized sports activity or a spontaneously-planned "very-little-sleep over," these are golden opportunities for middle-school girls to make contact and form community.

Not Time Sensitive
An important thing to remember is: effective communities don't have to last forever. Parents and teacher of middle-school girls must remember that these girls have only been alive for 11-14 years. Most teachers and all parents are more than twice their age. We adults need to remember that we have had at least twice the years on this planet than have our middle school charges; and while these girls are just now tip-toeing across the threshold of adulthood, we parents and teachers have been operating in the adult world for many, many years. So, what feels like a "long time" to a twelve year-old, may seem like tiny moment to adults.

Einstein may have gotten the credit for reminding us that time is relative; but for the parent or teacher of a middle-school boy or girl, the reminder comes almost every day. For example:
• For a middle-school girl, anyone 15-years older than she is, is old. Period. Thirty year-olds are old. Not as old as grandparents, perhaps; but old, nonetheless.
• If a trip to the beach is a week away, it can feel like light-years away to a 12 year-old.
• For a twelve year-old, when a best-friend ditches you or when someone makes fun of you, it can be one of the most devastating things that can ever happen in this life; and the pain (which parent and teacher know will soon pass) feels to the 12 year-old as if it will lasts forever.
• For a parent or teacher, to have a 12 year-old daughter or student win a sports trophy, get a top grade in school or get elected class treasurer, may bring a happy smile; but for the 12 year-old, it can feel like the achievement of a lifetime.

Time is utterly relative. That is a fact. And, when it comes to understanding and relating to a middle-schooler, there are few more important facts to keep in mind. Community experiences do not have to last years or even months. Longer community experiences definitely have their rewards; but even short-term events (volunteering with peers in some sort of community service, car washes and bake sales with other kids to raise money for a significant cause, regular get-togethers of peers to plan a special event, a family outing to which 3-4 middle-school friends are invited) can provide valuable community experiences and irreplaceable connections. Even the smallest community for the shortest period of time can offer priceless and long-lasting feelings of being accepted and worthy.

Never should we parents and teachers underestimate even the shortest-term community experience. When it comes to age, time is – and will forever be – relative. As comedian, George Carlin, was quoted as saying, "Quality of life is not measured by the number of breaths we breathe; but by the moments that take our breath away." Those breath-taking moments in community can enhance quality of life as nothing else can.

Uniforms and Community

Years before Hanger Hall School opened its doors, we explored the efficacy and problems of requiring uniforms. We talked with educators at independent and public schools who had experience with uniforms. And what we discovered was that in every case - make that every case we unearthed – the educators with whom we spoke were very clear that uniforms unquestionably helped more than they hindered. Uniforms, we were told, added to the school experience far more than detracting from it. The only negative issue that we heard regarding uniforms came from educators who had to transform a non-uniform school into a uniform school. "The struggle of trying to convince parents of the value of uniforms," said one school administrator, "nearly killed us. And, interestingly enough," she added, "it was the parents who professed more liberal politics and progressive educational techniques, who resisted the most."

Hanger Hall School does require uniforms for all students. And the dominant reasons for this decision came from school administrators who had years of experience with uniforms. The reasons are these:

- Uniforms eliminate any dress code questions. You're either in uniform or you're not - no length of dress to consider. No bra straps to deal with. No exposed belly to think about. No baggy pants to judge.
- Uniforms encourage self-expression from the inside out. Since you can't wear something you got from the mall to express your identity, then writing, speaking and behavior becomes the most important way of letting others know who you are. Students at Hanger Hall are constantly reminded by the teachers and by seeing everyone in uniforms, that individual expression and communicating personal identity is prized and valued at the School.
- Uniforms are easy. They are easy for the parents and easy for the students. When you know what you're wearing each day, getting dressed takes very little time.
- Uniforms level the fashion-playing field. No one can out-style anyone else.
- Uniforms help level the economic playing field. No one can wear a more expensive shirt or jacket than anybody else. Everybody knows how much everyone else's clothes cost, since they all cost the same.

But the reason that sold us entirely on the value of uniforms came from a principal in Oklahoma City who said, "Uniforms say 'welcome' to every new student." Uniforms say – subconsciously – that if you're in the uniform, you're part of the group. You are already accepted and already connected. Uniforms say, "You don't have to prove yourself. You are already part of the team. You are included."

This Oklahoma principal told us that when they started wearing uniforms in her K-5 school, it almost eliminated criers in kindergarten and 1st grade. "Normally," she said, "elementary schools have to deal with crying, homesick children for the first several weeks of the school year. With uniforms," she added, "when the children first show up and see that everyone is dressed like they were, there is almost no resistance and very little crying. "It is if," the principal said, "the children feel immediately accepted and part of the group." Translated: Uniforms help establish community. Uniforms provide subtle, but solid, connection to one another and to the school.

Some of the girls at Hanger Hall, of course, love to hate their uniforms. The 8th graders love to make jokes about them. The parents of the 6th graders, however, tell us that their daughters are so proud of their uniforms that they often refuse to take them off even at home, and sometimes they even sleep in them.

Our guess about this shift in attitude from 6th – 8th grades is that the 8th graders have already found a strong sense of community in the school, while the 6th graders sense that their uniforms are guaranteed tickets to that community. The 6th graders treasure the uniforms because they seek that connection and community.

Teachers Need Community Too

A rule of thumb for good business management is this: Always treat your employees as if they were your best clients. A highly respected and well-treated employee will create many, many good clients. Likewise, for schools: highly respected and well-treated teachers and parents will create many, many happy and successful students.

At Hanger Hall School, we have a saying: A happy teacher is a happy teacher. Meaning: happiness is crucial. And one of the best ways to keep a happy teacher happy is to follow the same community guideline as for the students. A happy teacher feels respected, accepted and connected. A happy teacher is one who feels that, in the company of the other teachers, she is at home - that her presence there in the school means more than simply doing her job. A happy teacher senses that she, herself, is 1) integral to the community, 2) trusted implicitly, and 3) that her thoughts, feelings and emotions are respected.

At Hanger Hall School, we offer a once-a-month Teachers' Night Out. The teachers are treated each month to drinks and dinner with no agenda other than having some fun. Needless to say, the teachers look forward to these dinner parties. And from these gatherings has developed an amicable camaraderie and delight which may not make showing-up early each morning at school and dealing with troublesome children (or parents) any easier; but it certainly takes the edge off.

And Parents…

One of the pits into which schools fall, again and again, is the pit called "trying to be all things to all people." One thing that school administrators learn early on is that you cannot and will not ever, ever, ever please every parent. It simply won't happen. Nor is it a school's job to provide everything every parent needs. If they're old enough to be parents, they're old enough to take care of themselves.

At the same time, when a parent feels like he or she is part of the school community rather than simply the guardian of a student who goes there, wonderful things happen. Projects get underwritten. Volunteers show up. And the spirit of the school lifts and flies.

Schools can offer social events, athletic events, parent/teacher council events, art and music events till the cows come home and still never truly develop a solid sense of community. When a parent comes to a school event, it is often simply to watch his or her child do something, not to feel a connection to or acceptance by the other parents. However, a school simply offering times for parents to gather is often enough. A school may not be able to actually create community for parents; but a school can provide lots of soil in which community may develop.

At Hanger Hall, during the summer, we have pool parties at a private pool. All school families are invited to these parties. The parties are pot-luck events. The families are encouraged to bring food to share. The school provides plates, cups and beverages. And though there is no directive (or even suggestion) in this regard, inevitably what happens is that the kids swim, eat, swim, eat and swim some more while the parents talk, eat, talk, eat and talk some more. The result is, that even before the first day of class in the fall, the parents have started to form community with each other and with the teachers and staff.

Likewise, it is important for parents to remember that they can foster school community as well. As parents of children, they are just as capable as school administrators of offering some parent-community-building events. Several of the parents at Hanger Hall, for example, started a tailgate coffee time in the parking lot during each Monday morning drop-off time. Parents who were not in a rush could park their cars, have a little coffee and chat a bit with other parents. Not everybody was interested, of course, or had the time. But each tailgate day, there might be 10-12 parents simply enjoying each others' company and sharing stories.

One thing is sure, however - parents are the most visible role model that a child has. Simply watching how parents move through life has a great deal to do with the choices their children will make. More than lectures, more than religious teaching, more than threats or bribes or any kind of supposed behavior modification techniques… more than any of these, a parent's example has, far and away, the most potency and effectiveness in teaching a child how to live. So, if the parents find and enjoy community somewhere, somehow, and on a regular basis, there is a very good chance that the children will follow suit.

Community Will Be Found

A big mistake parents and teachers often make is in thinking that children will not or cannot access what they need on their own. Part of a middle-school girl's necessary development is the ability to begin making choices on her own and to begin discovering for herself what she needs for survival and happiness. It is vital for a girl at this age to begin identifying how she is different - and therefore how her wants and needs are different - from Mom, Dad, teachers, friends and personalities she has met in literature and the media.

Community helps this identity development happen. Community assists this expansion into maturity and is, therefore, a fundamental need for a middle school girl. So, if she can't find community in school, church, clubs, friends or athletics, the chances are she will find or create it somehow. And some of these results may not be so pretty.

Teen gangs are a strong form of community. A gang provides for its members what any other community provides: acceptance, purpose and connection. Sometimes, the mere fact of a gang's illicit nature gives more strength to its existence. If a community has a common enemy, it binds that community more tightly together and makes it even more emotionally difficult for the members to drop out. A child who has not found community elsewhere is a prime candidate for membership in a gang. Hence, the need for parents and educators to help provide community.

Drugs or alcohol can also be rallying points for the creation of community. Getting together to get high also provides acceptance, purpose and connection. Drugs can become even a sacramental link to a sense of holiness or other-worldliness. If a child is struggling at school or home or with friends, she may relish the feeling of getting away that drugs offer, and at the same time enjoy the acceptance of the other users.

Now, wise parents and teachers are keenly aware that, with drugs and alcohol, experimentation is not the same as dependence. Trying and testing the waters around her is one of the most important self-development tasks a girl can do. And, it is ever so important that parents and teachers be open and ready for conversation in this arena. Coming down too hard on a girl who has experimented with the world of drugs or alcohol can often drive that girl even deeper into that world. But, when adults stick their heads in the sand and hide in denial, they are doing themselves and their middle-school girls a huge disfavor.

One of the challenges in our society is clearly that adults often use alcohol as a centerpiece for community. When children see adults getting sloshed at parties or constantly hear about "getting together for a drink," the message is clear: alcohol is a way of getting connected. Alcohol is a way of feeling welcome and at home. And this message can be highly detrimental to a middle-school girl who is seeking for anything or anyone who can help her get herself connected - to find her place in the world. Once again, the need for community is deeply rooted in the conscious and sub-conscious worlds of middle-school girls; and these girls will, more than likely, find community for themselves, be it healthy or destructive.

Creating Community

So, how do we create healthy community for our emerging adults? First, it's important to remember that you don't have to be a human relations expert, life coach or motivational guru to create community. Community happens naturally as long as a few of the key elements are present. Like planting a garden, community requires certain elements to grow. Gardens need soil, water, seeds and sun. Community needs people and purpose, collaboration and consensus. And remember, just having fun can be your purpose as well as the pivot point for consensus.

At Hanger Hall, we are constantly exploring ways to build community.
Here are a few that have worked for us:

- **Summer Pool Parties** – (Mentioned above) During each summer, we offer 3-4 pool parties to which all Hanger Hall students, alumni, teachers and administrators are invited. It's a family affair. Parents are invited to bring pot-lucky foods; and for a couple of hours, we have chatter and splashing, eating and laughing. New students get to meet each other as well as the older students. Parents get to talk with each other and to teachers… to discover which families live where… to discuss car-pooling or student's personalities and hobbies.
- **Camp** – Before classes begin each fall, all incoming and ongoing students, faculty and administrators check in at a camp just outside the city. We stay for 4 days and 3 nights. We do all the things you do at summer camp: canoe, swim, rock climb,

ropes course, horse-back riding, arts & crafts, sing-alongs, eating and sleeping together, talent shows, get-to-know-you games. We also do an initiation ceremony involving a waterfall – an initiation that was developed by students in the past for the new students.

- **Group** – (Mentioned several times throughout this book) Group is a time for the entire school to get together to talk about whatever the entire school needs to know. The subject can be schedules, field trip announcements and protocol. We might introduce visiting parents or students or discuss issues that have come up. We practice speaking, listening and social skills at group. We learn something about whatever religious holiday is being celebrated somewhere in the world and learn a bit about the religion. We celebrate birthdays and share important events in which one or more of the girls are involved. We celebrate sports victories and defeats, club projects, recent student discoveries and grieve together in the deaths of grandparents, close relatives or pets.

- **Advisor/Advisee** Early in each school year, every girl gets to choose a teacher whom she wants as her advisor. Not every girl gets her first choice, of course; but the point of choosing an advisor is to form a teacher/student connection that goes beyond classroom and academics. Each teacher advisor may have 4-6 advisees, and this group gets together on a regular basis just to "talk about things." There may be a specific agenda; but, more often than not, advisor/advisee time is simply a time to chat together. Sometimes, a teacher will take her advisees out to lunch or to a movie. Sometimes they go camping together or spend the night at the teacher's home. The value of the dynamic connections that form in these groups cannot ever be underestimated.

- **Travel** – A crucial piece in Hanger Hall's personal development. We are convinced that one of the best ways to empower young, emerging women, is to take them out of their comfort and enable them to actually experience another place… another way of life… another way of thinking. There is absolutely nothing like traveling together that can build community and self-esteem at the same time. (See Chapter 9)

- **Travel Group** – A vital aspect of promoting personal growth at Hanger Hall is our travel program. When we travel together as classes or as the entire school, we have Group every morning and night. Topics of discussion are generally what happened that day and what we learned from it. Often at Travel Group, we ask the girls to write a poem or sing a song about what they discovered about the place we are visiting or what they discovered about themselves that day.
- **Ritual** – One of the main things that keep religious communities together is the regular practice of ritual. Whether it be a Passover Meal for those of Jewish tradition, Communion or Eucharist for the Christian, Sangha for the Buddhist or Satsang for the Hindu, participation in regular ritual together helps create community in ways that little else can. Hanger Hall is not a religious school in the sense of advocating a certain religious tradition, though we do learn about and honor world religions.

There are cultural rituals, however, which can have much of the same effect as the religious variety. At Hanger Hall, we 1) regularly celebrate birthdays by wearing a birthday crown, singing and eating some form of cake together. We 2) do an initiation of all new students. We 3) do a ritual at graduation which includes lighted candles and the passing of the light of leadership from 8th to 7th graders. At the end of every Group, we 4) cross arms and hold hands in a circle to recite The Hanger Hall Pledge. Likewise, 5) when we travel together, every day we offer what we call "Sky Lake Vitamins," which is nothing but whipped cream that is squirted directly into the mouth. And the ritual rule is that no one can squirt it into her own mouth. It has to be done by another student or teacher. Regularly practiced cultural rituals - even silly ones – can bind a group together
- **Adventure Club** – Several parents at The School came up with this idea; and it works wonderfully well! Each week, an e-mail goes out to all students notifying them of an upcoming "adventure." It can be horseback riding, whitewater rafting, hiking to a waterfall, boating, waterskiing, snow skiing, rock climbing. Or sometimes, it's just going out for a pizza together. Not everyone participates in every adventure, but the cumulative effect on the School is fantastic community building.

All the students know all the rituals. So, simply by doing these rituals on a regular basis brings us closer together as a community. When we do these rituals we all feel connected. The rituals help define who we are as a community. So many ways to build community, so little time!

The Circle Dance – Ancient Wisdom
The circle dance is one of the oldest and most common dances throughout the world. Sometimes lively, sometimes slow and meditative, you can find circle dances in European, Middle Eastern, Asian, North/Central and South American traditions. Sometimes the circle dances are gender-specific. Women in Korea, for example have traditional circle dances for the harvest. Likewise in Greek tradition, dances are often for either men or women.

But gender-specific or not, circle dances are found throughout the world and have evidently been used since ancient times to celebrate the human experiences. The Guohuang dance from Tibet is done to celebrate births, battle victories and weddings. Batuque is an African/South American dance around a solo dancer who shows his or her stuff and then changes places with another in the circle. Many Native American tribes dance in circles for their traditional Pow-wows. The Hora is a dance of Romanian and Middle Eastern tradition primarily used at weddings and is almost always danced by everyone present. Sufi Whirling or Dervish Dancing has the dancers spinning individually in a circle. Even the Merengue, which is today performed by couples, was originally a Caribbean Island circle dance.

No one knows the origin of the circle dance. It may well be that our species' earliest rituals and festivals were performed – by necessity – around a fire, making the circle dance a natural. But, it may also be that circle dances were a way of bringing the tribe or clan together and celebrating the connection-to, and need-for, each other.

When you stand, sit or dance in a circle, you can see every face and everybody. Being in a circle offers the obvious and subliminal message that 1) you are part of something; 2) you are part of something greater than yourself; and 3) that you are accepted and welcome here just as you are.

Another clear message of the circle dance, as you move around in whichever direction, is that you never stay where you started. You're always moving into a new place - a possibly unfamiliar place. But, no matter where you are in the circle, you are always part of the circle. As a potent life metaphor, this reminder can have a compelling impact on each dancer and on the community of dancers as a whole.

For people of all ages, but particularly for middle school girls, this is a huge and convincing lesson. Middle school girls are going through dramatic changes: physical changes, emotional changes, social changes, psychological, mental, spiritual and moral changes. And as we all know, any kind of change in any part of our lives can disrupt nearly everything in the rest of our lives. The middle school years are some of the most convoluted, confusing and elaborately complex years of change that humans go through in a lifetime.

Hence, the need for the message of the circle dance: No matter where you are or what you are going through,
1) You are part of something.
2) You are part of something greater than yourself.
3) You are accepted and welcome here just as you are. It's the message of the circle dance. It's the message of community.

If there is but one thing that we as parents and educators provide for our middle-school girls, and that one thing is healthy and happy community, then we have done a good thing. A very good thing.

Crucial Community

Two
STRUCTURE & FLEXIBILITY

Following the rules gives you more freedom. - Page, grade 7

Chaos and Order

Scientists and theologians love to argue about all kinds of things. Scientists love to argue and quarrel with each other. Within the theological community, it's the same thing. Get a scientist and a theologian together and it can become a verbal melee.

And one of the things both scientists and theologians like to argue about is chaos and order. Do we live in a chaotic universe or not? Is there an order which we cannot discern? Or is what we call "order" or "chaos" simply a human concept? Are there even such things as chaos or order? Some scientists and theologians claim that chaos can come from order and vice-versa. Some of us simply say, "Life is chaotic. Let's order a beer."

One thing we know: Living in society requires an ability to deal with both chaos and order. And this very lesson is one of the most important for middle-school girls to assimilate and understand.

You can't just have all structure or all flexibility because then, everything would be chaos.
- Neena , grade 7

The Chaos and Order Dance

The middle-school, pubescent years can feel utterly chaotic to a girl going through it, and often, even more chaotic to her parents and teachers. The radical and dramatic changes that are going on within a middle-school girl's body, in her thinking, her emotions – with all of these rapid and volcanic changes, a middle-school girl can feel totally out of control and without any order. And this can create windstorms of anxiety and tornadoes of fretfulness and fear in the landscape of any young, emerging woman.

Middle-schoolers need order. They need structure. A middle-school girl needs to know that even though her personal world feels tumultuous, confused and chaotic, the whole world is not that way. She needs a sense that there is something to hang on to. Some kind of anchor in the storm. Some kind of rock that will not get washed away.

Something as simple as a regular school schedule can provide that structure, or regular meal times, consistent parental love or a teacher's constancy in expectations. School uniforms provide excellent structure, as do report cards, dependable curfew times and holiday celebrations.

But, at the same time, middle-school girls need freedom. They need a sense of chaos… a comfort with spontaneity. Middle-school girls need to know that things are not always tied down, bound up, all nailed into place. Middle-school girls are deeply aware that everything within in them is changing – that life is slip-sliding around – and unless they have some freedom and chaos mixed in to their daily life, they can feel trapped. They can feel as if they are misfits: wildly changing beings in an unchanging world. Middle-school girls need to know that, though order exists, there is flexibility in the order. These girls need to know that chaos and order are dancing together.

Being cognizant of the chaos/order "dance" is another example of the onset abstract thinking (See Chapter 3). Developmentally, this happens in both boys and girls during puberty. However, as we have said before, girls are normally 2-3 years ahead of boys in their pubescent development. As a rule, an 11 year-old girl is capable of thinking with abstract concepts in ways that her male peers will not be able to do until they are 13-14 years old. A middle-school girl can talk or write about the chaos and order in her life. And, it's a pretty good idea to encourage that kind of talking and writing with these girls.

Bones and Muscle

On a physiological/ biological level, a middle school girl is the poster-children for the dance of chaos and order. Bones, which provide structure, are going through tremendous growth. Muscles and tendons, which provide flexibility and movement, are growing as well. Glands, which had lain dormant for 10-11 years, are now kicking into high gear and changing the inner and outer landscape of her body. And though there is order to the process, it is often a clumsy and chaotic kind of order. Bones seem to grow faster than the muscles around them. Muscles, which had been seldom used as a child, are now being stretched into new activity; and muscles and tendons which were used as a child, are now lying inactive. And combine that with the shift of body fat, growth of new hair and breasts and the onset of menstruation; growing pains are very real.

Awkwardness and Self-Consciousness

But, it's not just physical growing pains that a middle-school girl has to deal with. Physical growing pains are accentuated and heightened by emotional growing pains. The two can become a vicious circle. And as the result, a girl can feel uncomfortable in her own body. She can feel ill at ease just in being herself. All of sudden, this little girl who was so relaxed and content with herself for 8-10 years is now experiencing a new discomfort – a new sense of distress. And, if the girl is acting a bit awkward or clumsy, there's a good chance she is feeling the same way.

To say a middle-school girl is often self-conscious would be a bald faced understatement. Of course she is! She has every right to be! There's so much going on in her self to be conscious of. There's so much going on in the world around her and in the way she views the world. Self-consciousness comes naturally. But, when self-consciousness descends into anxious insecurity and profound embarrassment, a girl can retreat. She can pull inside and cut off communication for fear she will say something "stupid" or act in a brainless way.

This is precisely where the importance of small classes comes into play, especially, small, single gender classes. In the super-self-conscious phase of pubescent development, small, single-gender classes are a saving grace for the middle-school girl. With a small class, she doesn't feel as if she is performing for an audience every time she asks or answers a question. With a small class of all girls, she doesn't have to worry about sounding too smart or too stupid in front of the "cute" boy. At this age, with self-consciousness at an all-time high, the less that can intimidate… the less that can give the feeling that she's on stage and in the spotlight… the less she feels judged… and the more she feels connected to the classroom community, then the more the middle-school girl will participate, the more she'll assimilate and the less she'll fret.

Visitors to Hanger Hall School are constantly blown away by the quality and quantity of classroom participation. In small classrooms, of course, no one is on the back row because there is no back row. The class operates far more as a seminar than a lecture hall. No one can get lost, overlooked or ignored. Likewise, no student feels as if she's on stage, performing for an anonymous (and potentially jeering) audience.

With this awkward and self-conscious state, the need for parents and teachers to offer assurance and support is extraordinarily important. Nor should this support come with transparent, feel-good platitudes or emotional crutches: the let-me-do-it-for-you kind of thing. Most girls can see through those greeting-card style perk-me-up clichés. And, artificial emotional crutches of over-compensating assistance can give a very clear message that says, "You are not capable of handling this. I will do it for you." Rather than strengthening a girl with cliché wisdom and do-it-for-you crutches, you wind up debilitating her even more.

One of the best ways to offer assurance and support to a middle-school girl, is to let her know that all of life is a mix of chaos and order. All of life - every fragment and morsel – has its own orderliness and its own dis-order; and both are necessary for growth. If that message is conveyed again and again in both obvious and subtle ways, the chances are, that sooner or later, it will sink in and allow the girl to give herself some slack and realize that when she feels awkward or self-conscious, when she doesn't understand what's going on around or within her, doesn't understand why she feels the way she does, why she says what she says, why her friends and parents and teachers act so weird - when she feels as if life is either falling apart or way too restrictive, she's right on. She's fully alive and up to her eyeballs in the way life actually works.

Rules here are a bit flexible until it comes to Drama Class. Then, it's straight forward. Not. - **Hannah, grade 7**

Rules for School and Home

At school there are rules for everything: class schedules, field trip expectations, test days, report cards, dress code, lunchroom behavior. There are rules for promptness, politeness and quiet in the halls, rules for honesty and honor codes, integrity, term papers and plagiarism, rules about smoking or drinking or drugs, rules about sex or birth control or STD's. So many rules to follow - so much order, so much structure, so many policies and regulations, laws and directives.

Then, there's home - meal times, curfew times and time outs. There are rules for cell phones, TV's, computers and internet, rules for inside voice and outside voice. "How many friends can come over? How long can they stay? Can we eat in the bedroom?" There are rules for over-nighters, for day-trippers. There are rules for cleaning up your room, for emptying the dishwasher and taking out the trash. There are rules for study time, movie ratings, and behavior at meals. There are even rules for sleeping - when you start and when you stop. The rules go on and on - so many rules and regulations to consider, so many to keep track of, so many policies to follow.

Now, keep in mind that this mountain of restrictive order comes at a time when the girl child is feeling the first breezes of freedom. The rules come at a time when the girl is just beginning to be aware of what an astoundingly wide world of possibility there is out there. Not only is she becoming more and more aware of all kinds of life going on around her, but she is actually given the ability to grow new life within her. She now has – or soon will have - the ability to create, grow and have a baby!

And, of course, the rules come thick and fast during the middle-school years because we parents and teachers are fully aware of this emerging freedom and of our middle-schoolers' budding consciousness of limitless possibility. We authority figures watch our middle-school children as they discover new things, new attitudes, new ideas, new sensations. We watch them as they develop adult bodies and adult ways of thinking. We watch them begin to methodically cut the apron strings that have bound them to their parents and to the ways of their childhood. We watch them snip the tethers that have had them circling family and school. And, often from a desire to simply protect them – though sometimes from a deep sense of fear that we are losing them – we throw up rules and regulations around them so fast it can make their heads spin.

Spontaneity and Flexibility

No one, of course, likes to be caged. Especially those who are just beginning to discover freedom. And if we as parents and educators are not careful, we can, with our rules and regulations, give our young, emerging-adults the feeling that they are not trusted - that they (like wild animals) need to be caged with the walls and fences of rules, policies and structure.

When we took our first few extended trips as a school, we had some parents who were quite convinced that their daughters would try to sneak out of their hotel rooms as night and, more than likely, get into trouble. These parents proposed that we put electronic monitors in the rooms, tape on the doors or have adults sleeping across the inside of the hotel doors so there would be no chance of the girls sneaking out.

As faculty and staff, we listened to the parents' concerns; and then we talked with the girls. We told them of their parent's apprehension. We suggested that they talk with their parents and assure them that they would follow the school rules. We told them that, at Hanger Hall, we would rather trust than not trust. Therefore, rather than assuming that they would break the rules, we would rather assume that they were trustworthy. But, if they broke our trust, we made it quite clear that we would promptly send them home.

Over the years, with many, many extended school trips, we have never had to send a single student home. Sometimes trust is betrayed. Sometimes the high ideals get knocked down; but we feel strongly that starting with trust - beginning with high ideals – is always the best way to go.

Finding the balance between the need for order and flexibility can be ever-so challenging. At Hanger Hall, we encourage spontaneity in many arenas. Teachers, for example, have the option to take any class, at any time, on a spontaneous field trip. Parents sign off on this at the first of the year with a general permission slip for short, unplanned field trips. Since each class has no more than 12 students, it's easy for them all to pile into our 15-passenger van or bus and scoot out for a quick and un-scheduled trip to anywhere from the public library to an art gallery or a river side or an ice cream shop.

We have discovered that this kind of order-breaking spontaneity is productive on two levels: Academically, it opens the door for new ideas to break out in class, new questions to be asked, new enthusiasm for whatever subject may be at hand. In terms of community building, this kind of spontaneity is invaluable. It says loud and clear that school is for more than pounding information into your head. This spontaneity shouts that learning is not limited to a teacher's lesson plans; learning can happen spontaneously everywhere. This freedom teaches that orderly learning is only one way to learn, that unplanned things happen all the time in life and of course, this liberty teaches the biggie: that school can be fun. Learning to be spontaneous is one of the most valuable lessons parents and teachers can offer their emerging adults.

It is important, however, for parents to remember that their middle-school girl is now at the stage of life when she wants to start creating her own agenda. She wants to start putting together her own schedule. Eleven and twelve year-old girls are beginning to like the idea that they have some control over how they spend their days. So, on the one hand, it's a great idea for mom to show up in daughter's room at 5:00 in the afternoon and spontaneously announce, "Instead of having supper here, we're going out on a picnic and a moonlight hike. Get ready." On the other hand, Daughter may have already made plans for the evening. She might be planning a study session with a friend or planning to read or write in her journal. She may be expecting a phone call from a good buddy.

So, Mom & Dad, beware! The spontaneous idea may be greeted with a cheer. Or it may be greeted with a, "Do we have to? I have plans." You've learned the lesson a thousand times; but here it comes again, "Being a parent is 90% guesswork."

Clarity and Consistency
As we have already mentioned earlier in this chapter, because of all the changes going on in her life, a middle-school girl needs structure. She needs to know where the lines are drawn. And one of the best things that parents and teachers can do is to make those lines clear - to make sure that your daughter or student knows exactly what is expected, and when and why. Clarity is essential. If a girl doesn't know the rules - with all the details - she certainly can't be expected to follow them. And because, at this age, the rules are flying thick and fast, it is vital for the rules to be restated again and again.

At Hanger Hall, we have regular meetings of the entire student body, teachers and administrators. It's called "Group," (See Chapter 1) and its purpose is to build community and mutual understanding by talking through schedules and issues, making announcements, celebrating birthdays, practicing social skills, sharing observations and dealing with whatever has come up which involves the whole school.

And one of the things we do at Group on a regular basis, is to remind the students of "the way we do things at Hanger Hall." This reminder can be about all kinds of things in all kinds of areas. "The way we do things at Hanger Hall," reminder can involve uniforms, field trip behavior, plagiarism, eye contact, tardiness, absentee policy - whatever it may be. It can be rules, policies or expectations - whatever helps define who we are as a community. "The way we do things at Hanger Hall," may not be the way these girls do things with other organizations or at home. At church groups, they may be allowed to wear whatever they want. At home, they may be able to use their cell phones. But, "at Hanger Hall," they are reminded, "we do things a certain way." And we have discovered that the clearer we are, and more times we remind (re – mind) each other of how we operate, then the less confused, the more comfortable and relaxed we can all be.

Consistency is also a vital aspect of the order. If a rule changes every week or gets interpreted differently by Mom and Dad or from one teacher to another, the rule is worthless. The message is of rule changing becomes: there is no order here, only subjective ideas. If you want to undermine a middle-school girl's sense of stability, start messing with the rules. Be lax with some and strict with others, or ignore a rule one week and lay it down hard the next.

All children need limits. They need to know where the boundaries are. They need to know that certain things happen in certain ways for certain reasons. They need to have the sense that life can be trusted. They need to know that there are people, places and situations on which they can depend. This is absolutely vital for a child to be able to grow and operate with any kind of confidence, security and ease. When a child grows up in a world in which nothing is certain, where nothing can be trusted, where everything is haphazard, random, chaotic, then the defense mechanisms kick in big-time. And, as a result, the child learns to live defensively, always doing battle or ready to do battle with the unexplained and unexplainable. This child becomes a candidate for gangs who offer protection, drugs which offer escape, and crime, since rules don't count and laws are worthless. We do our middle-school girls a huge disadvantage when we fail to offer clear, consistent rules and limits for daily living.

Changing the Rules
Not that the rules can't change. Not that expectations can't be modified. The very act of altering policies and regulations helps a middle-school girl understand that life is always changing and that rules can change with it. But, if a rule is to be changed, it needs to be discussed: How are we changing? Why are we changing? And when will the change begin?

We had a suggestion come up several years ago at Hanger Hall that the 8th graders be allowed, "free dress day" every now and then. Up until that time, uniforms were required at school every day and at every school event, including field trips. The suggestion (coming, of course, from an 8th grader) was that every so often, we should allow the "senior" students the privilege of choosing what they would wear.

So, the teachers and administration decided to let this be the topic for one of our Forums. Forum happens every Thursday after lunch. It is a time for the whole school to discuss ideas and issues in some depth. We let the 8th graders know that we would have an open discussion of the possible rule change and that we would expect them to have one or more spokespersons who could defend the reasons for the rule change.

There was a whirlwind of activity and excitement among the 8th graders in preparing their case; in the meantime, we challenged the 6th and 7th graders to come up with questions to ask the 8th graders about the idea of free dress: Could they wear anything they wanted? Pajamas? Swim suit? Did they have to do something good to earn free dress? How often could they have free dress? Could we possibly extend free dress to the whole school every now and then? Etc.

So, at Free Dress Forum Day, we began by restating why Hanger Hall requires uniforms: How uniforms encourage self-expression from the inside out and discourage distraction by keeping fashion statements out of the classroom. We talked about how uniforms help to level the playing field and help us all to feel good about ourselves by not allowing any girl from a wealthy home to dress better than someone who can't afford expensive clothes.

Then, we opened it up to the 8th graders who had prepared written defenses of their position and had even collected signatures on a petition from most of the students in the school. Their arguments included: 1) since the 8th graders had been with the school longer than the 6th and 7th graders, they should have special recognition; 2) if Hanger Hall was trying to teach girls to be strong and think for themselves, this potential variation in our rules was a fine example of just that; and 3) allowing 8th graders to have a free dress day every now and then would make all the younger students excited about studying hard and getting to be an 8th grader.

Then, came the questions from the 6th and 7th graders: Why was this fair? If 8th graders could have free dress, why not everybody? What kind of dress code would they have to follow? If a visitor came to the school on free dress day, what would they think? And so on.

The administration and faculty listened to all the promotion, defense and questions; and at the end of Forum, told the students that they would meet and make a decision within the week. And a week later, it was announced that 1) the 8th graders could have one free dress day a month; 2) they would have to wear something that their parents would allow if they were going downtown as a family; 3) if there were any disruptive behavior as the result of a free dress day, it would be cancelled for the next month.

And so, the former every-day-is-uniform-day policy got changed. And it was clear and clean. And everyone understood that rules can change; but that order still exists.

Care and Compassion

But just as important as order and flexibility, a child must learn that there is forgiveness - that mistakes are made - mistakes with order and mistakes with spontaneity. Middle-school girls need to know that no one can follow all the rules all the time. No one can operate spontaneously and not do something stupid every now and then. Girls need to know that, right along with the limits and the flexibility, there is care and compassion. An emerging adult needs to know that flexibility and rules are there because human life is precious – that her life is precious - and flexibility and rules are there to protect and enhance that life.

In order to develop a confidence in her self in a sometimes chaotic world, a middle-school girl needs to know that even when she makes stupid choices, the world does not fall apart. Even when order gets shattered and spontaneity gets abused, life can - and does - go on.

An unexpected family death can shatter a child's belief in the constancy of life. It can annihilate faith in any kind of order in the world. If a girl's parents get divorced, the very upheaval of family and home can be devastating and leave emotional scars for years. Hence, the need to assimilate and even embrace chaos. A middle-school girl needs to know that no matter how many rules and regulations get put in place, crazy things still happen. Random events and accidents are common. Chance occurrences and unanticipated incidents happen all the time. As the old adage goes: Life is what happens after you've made your plans. Or, like the Yiddish proverb: You know how to make God laugh? Tell Him your plans. Just as important as instilling a respect for limits, it is vital for parents and teachers to encourage an awareness and even an embrace of the chaotic nature of life.

And that is precisely where care and compassion enter the picture. When life comes apart at the seams, when things that shouldn't be happening start happening, when nothing makes sense and the world around you collapses, that's where compassion and care become irreplaceable.

Care and compassion do not make up for the unpleasant chaos in life. Care and compassion offer no magic wand to make the chaos go away. Offering care and compassion is a bit like singing the blues. When you sing about your hard times, it doesn't necessarily change the way things are, but it helps you name the problems, face the problems and know that somehow, you'll get through them. And just as singing always beats the heck out of moaning and groaning, care and compassion can help any of us get through the hard times better.

The word "compassion" comes from the Latin words, *cum pasio:* literally, "with suffering." In most cases, the absolutely best thing you can do when someone is suffering is to be with them. Simply being with someone who is hurting, holding her hand and listening with full attention just might be the most healing and helpful medicine in the world.

It's All About Balance

Too much chaos can make you crazy. Too much order can bore you to tears. The pendulum in our daily lives keeps swinging back and forth from order to chaos to order and back again.

When our days follow the same pattern over and over and over with the same job, same people, same routine, same bills, same worries, same TV programs, same dinner times, same sleep cycle, same weekend activities… when our lives start to feel canned, programmed and on automatic pilot, we often want to run out and do something crazy. We want to go parasailing or bungee-jumping or water-skiing or simply go on vacation to a place we've never been. One of the reasons so often given for having extra-marital affairs is simply, "I was bored in my marriage." It is, indeed, possible to have too much order in our lives.

But, the reverse is true, as well. If every day is frenetic: running here, running there… having to stop what you're doing to attend to this or that… having to stop doing this or that to run somewhere else… people dropping in with no appointments…. no schedule… no plan… no agenda… when everything in your day feels unexpected and unanticipated with no clear goals or objectives, it can make you run screaming for a steady relationship, a placid home life and a 9-5 job at the library.

There are some biologic research scientists who say that life requires chaos and order to even get started. From the onset of life on earth to the dance of Mr. Sperm and Ms. Egg, some contend that a healthy mix of chaos and order is required. Evolutionary biology is the study of how random events somehow come together to form some sort of order either as the result of natural selection or the particular requirements of a species. In any event, researchers in biology along with every teacher or parent whoever paid attention know that order and chaos are part and parcel of every part of creation, part of every child who ever lived. And, the opportunity of learning to live with order and chaos on a daily basis may be one of the most important abilities we can offer our middle-school girls.

- Three -
THINKING ABOUT THINKING

I love thinking about thinking; but, it confuses me completely. - Ellen, grade 7

"What in the world was she thinking?!" is a lament frequently heard by parents of middle-school girls. Jean Piaget (pronounced pee-ah-jay; 1896-1980) made an earnest and sweeping attempt to answer that question during the early to middle 20th century.[1]

Piaget was a Swiss scientist-philosopher who spent a lifetime sorting out how kids know what they know. In the process, he developed a unique set of mini-tests using common objects found any American home. No #2 pencils for Piaget! He used things like pennies (more probably Swiss francs), balls of clay and beakers of colored liquid. Nor did he count up the number of correct answers and turn it into a percentage. Piaget wanted to know how kids came up with their answers, regardless of whether the answer was "right" or "wrong."

Stage Theory and Piaget

Psychologists call Piaget a stage theorist. Stage theorists generally agree on several points. First, they believe that children (and adults) move from one stage to another according to a defined sequence. Stage 1 is first, stage 2 comes next, etc. Knowledge acquired during the earlier stages serves as the foundation for later stages.

Second, stage theorists generally assign age ranges to each stage. These age ranges are not fixed in stone, but there is often an assumption that children move relatively quickly (over the course of a few weeks or months) from one stage to another. Finally, most stage theorists believe that their proposed stages are somewhat universal. It is assumed, to some extent, that everyone progresses through the same stages, in the same order, at roughly the same ages around the world.

As you might imagine, researchers disagree about the usefulness of stage theories. Some think that the assigned ages are either slightly inaccurate or flat out incorrect. Others think that cultural differences make universal theories about anything highly unlikely. And there are many researchers who are pretty sure that development doesn't occur in stages at all! Nevertheless, stage theories often provide useful guidelines about what types of behaviors and thought processes we might expect to observe during different points in development. And many of psychology's most influential thinkers put forth stage theories.

Piaget was one of them. His theory greatly advanced our understanding of how children think about the world around them; and he did so at a time when children were not widely studied. His ideas have also helped shape individual classroom practice and overall educational systems throughout the world. In contemplating the joys and challenges and adventures associated with the middle school years, Piaget's theory offers several valuable themes.

Sensorimotor Stage: 0-2 Years

At some point, every stage theorist has to settle on how many stages there are. Piaget chose four. The first stage, from age 0-2 years, is called the Sensorimotor Stage. Ever notice how infants touch everything? Sucking, biting, banging, throwing, dropping, and kicking all provide great sources of amusement. According to Piaget, however, it's more than entertainment. This is how infants and toddlers learn about their world.

When infants swipe their bowl of Cheerios off the high chair tray, they learn that objects fall to the ground and sometimes break. When infants put objects in their mouths, they learn about texture. When infants bang objects, they learn about softness and hardness. All of this "play" behavior also teaches children to make connections between how something looks and how it feels. It may be a nightmare for parents in the Hallmark store, but it's great for cognitive development.

Preoperational Stage: 2-7 Years

The second stage, from age 2-7 years, is called the Preoperational Stage. Obviously, children learn a variety of fascinating tricks during these years. Parents of preschoolers love to sit around and share stories about potty-training, drawing abilities, and block-building talents. During the early school years, parents watch in fascination as their young children learn to write letters, sound out words, and add simple sums. For Piaget, one of the highlights of this developmental period was an emerging understanding of symbols, that one thing stands for something else.

Vocabulary development provides a great example. Children learn that particular words, like "cat" or "dog," represent particular types of four-legged, furry animals. And once again, it's easy to see that toddlers love to practice their newly emerging skills. Kids repeat nearly everything, including the occasional swear word. They also point to objects and expect them to be labeled. When my daughter was 2, she used to wake up and immediately start naming everything she saw – ball, doll, book, window, Mommy. And she once spent an entire day whispering the word "imaginary" over and over again.

This is also perhaps why children love to pretend. Pretending relies on an understanding of symbols. Bedroom slippers become trucks, beautiful dolls become light sabers, and battered books become imaginary guests at a tea party. Children this age also easily create elaborate and magical fantasy worlds. Dragons, unicorns, princesses, and superheroes all spin tales in enchanted forests, castles, spaceships, and submarines.

Like the banging of toys and the naming of objects, pretending provides children with the practice they need to gain important knowledge about the world around them. This knowledge will then become the foundation for more complicated abilities. Children don't know this, of course; they just know that it's fun to pretend.

And therein lies the real beauty of cognitive development. There might be a better way to master symbolic representation, but it's difficult to think of a way that would be more enjoyable.

Despite all this playful practice and the increased brain-power that comes with it, it's still fairly easy to trick a young child. If you break a cookie into two halves, young children will often think they have more. Shadows are living beings, and they are fairly sure that the moon is following them. Piaget suggested that these thoughts occur because young children actually perceive the world differently from adults.

In one study, a researcher put a dog mask on her pet cat, Maynard.[2] Early in the preoperational stage (around age 3-4), most children were fairly certain that Maynard had now become a barking, fetching, dog-chow-eating canine. The realization that Maynard was still a cat that happened to be wearing a dog mask didn't occur until about age 5 or 6. Young children are also quite certain that the information in their brains is exactly the same as the information in everyone else's brain. If Maynard has now become a dog, then Maynard has become a dog to everyone. Such findings do indeed suggest that young minds are frolicking on a slightly different playground.

Concrete Operations Stage: 7-11 Years

The third stage, from age 7-11 years, is called the Concrete Operations Stage. (Feeling relieved that you aren't reading this in the original French?) These ages roughly correspond to grades 1-6, which includes beginning middle-schoolers. During these years, the distance between appearance and reality widens. The broken stick is somewhat less likely to "be" a telephone, and the frightening monster mask at Halloween is recognized as just a costume. Language play becomes more complex. Rhyming games and knock-knock jokes are babyish. Corny riddles, jump rope jingles, and hand clapping games are cool. Metaphors begin to make sense, making it fun to practice emerging language skills through poetry and short stories. And maps become simultaneously more symbolic and more decipherable.

Games begin to have rules during this stage, and inventing those rules is part of the fun. Take, for example, my daughter and her friends at the local swimming pool. The original game consisted of one girl in the pool throwing a ball at one girl jumping off the side. This evolved into the requirement that the girl take a running leap off the side. (Well, a fast-walking leap, thanks to the lifeguards.) This evolved into the requirement that the girl "do a trick" while taking a fast-walking leap. And this necessitated a point system for tricks and catches. All these rules emerged in a matter of minutes.

Knowledge about concrete operations also provides valuable clues about teaching social skills (See Chapter 7). Hanger Hall is definitely not a "finishing school," but they recognize that social skills can instill confidence and self-assurance. At Hanger Hall, social skills are not simply discussed; they are acted out. Students engage in role-play. They watch other students model both appropriate and inappropriate social responses. They are reminded and encouraged to practice their social skills in real-word situations, whenever the occasion arises. All of these exercises are intended to make social skills concrete, to place them firmly within the cognitive grasp of even the youngest girls at the school.

One of the hallmarks of Concrete Operations is that logical thinking emerges. Objects can now be placed into categories, hierarchies, and groups. The concept of animals can be subdivided into dogs, cats, fish, and birds. The concept of dogs can be further subdivided into terriers, poodles, and beagles. Terriers can be further divided into Jack Russell, Irish, and Fox. Mastery is gained through sorting. Over and over again. In innumerable different ways. Rocks, feathers, and bracelets can be sorted by color, shape, size, color and shape, or shape and size. And then they can be sorted again! Parents, teachers, and classmates can also be sorted – smart and bossy, creative and athletic, dramatic and sullen. As a result, the social world becomes increasingly complex.

During Concrete Operations, children also learn that perspectives vary from person to person. For example, they know that if I stand on one side of a sculpture and they stand on the other side, we see different versions of the same piece of art. They also know that thoughts, opinions, ideas, and feelings vary from person to person.

A regular activity at Hanger Hall is called "Observations." During "Observations," the girls are invited to share something of what they have observed in the world around them. There are two parameters: 1) It must something actually observed by the individual speaking, and 2) It must be described briefly, preferably in three sentences or less. The girls love Observations. They love the chance to think about what they have seen and describe it to others. It can be a movie they watched, something to do with their pet, something their parents said or did, a blooming lily, the taste of asparagus… anything. The challenge to condense that observation into a pithy, articulate, and understandable statement is something they all love doing. The game of Observations helps them realize that they are observing and differentiating the various parts of their world; and that each person sees things differently.

Finally cultural differences now take on new meaning. Learning about the kinds of clothes that others wear or the kind of food that others eat or the kind of games that others play is fascinating for children of this age. Books, television, and movies all provide outlets for practicing these new mental skills in a playful fashion. Family vacations and school trips are even better – flooding the senses with similarities and differences that can be contemplated, sorted, and discussed. As you will see in Chapters 6 and 9, Hanger Hall places special emphasis on travel, in part because of the cognitive skills travel can promote.

Despite the obvious cognitive advances taking place, overall thinking during Concrete Operations happens with information in the here and now, with life data that is experienced personally. This is one of the reasons why experiential learning is so powerful during the elementary and early middle school years. At Hanger

Hall, lessons are regularly taught through games, bodily movement, and activation of all the senses (See Chapter 10). Students of all ages can certainly benefit from this approach to teaching, but for children still in Concrete Operations, it may be a necessity.

Soon however, additional learning strategies will become effective. According to Piaget, another important transition is on the horizon. This transition happens around puberty. Because girls go through puberty slightly earlier than boys, girls are poised to make yet another important mental leap during the precious middle school years. An essential component in any middle school's mission should therefore be helping girls to navigate this life-changing cognitive transition to adulthood.

Formal Operations: Puberty through Adulthood

The leap to Piaget's fourth and final stage, Formal Operations, is marked by increases in at least three sets of abilities – reasoning abstractly, reflecting on multiple perspectives, and solving complex problems systematically. As with all the other stages, it's fun to practice these newfound mental skills, and Hanger Hall provides a constant flow of creative, fun ways to exercise the mind. Since it is in Formal Operations that most middle-school girls find themselves - or need to be finding themselves – it is important to examine this stage a bit more closely.

Sometimes when I'm thinking about thinking, I forget to remember. –Paige, grade 7

Formal Operations: Reasoning Abstractly

Abstract concepts are difficult, if not impossible, to experience directly through the senses. Faith, beauty, evil, and justice are examples. Certainly children in Concrete Operations are familiar with these words. They can tell stories about people being bad or acting unfairly. They can also identify items or people that are beautiful. But Piaget believed that only older children could really understand such terms as purely mental concepts – without having to resort to specific, concrete examples.

This ability opens new worlds to young adolescents. They suddenly find it fascinating to reflect on morality and religion. They become frustrated by perceived injustices. They can imagine a future full of possibilities. They can ponder impossible situations.

Hanger Hall provides frequent opportunities for such mental exercise. Life often requires a bit of tight-rope walking. We all must strike a balance between rigidity and flexibility, between seriousness and fun, or between pride and humility (See Chapter 2). Being able to contemplate that balance, however, is a skill largely reserved for those in Formal Operations. At Hanger Hall, daily life is mostly structured. Ninety percent of any given school day goes according to an established schedule. Certain classes are offered in certain rooms at certain times by certain teachers. Lunch is at the same hour every day. Uniforms are required during all school hours and at all school activities.

But, the students at Hanger Hall also know that almost anything is possible. Parents give permission at the beginning of the school year for spur-of-the-moment field trips. On pretty days, you'll see many of the teachers taking their classes outside. If a really important issue comes up (good or bad), we might take all students out of class and get them together somewhere for a short, impromptu Group. A free dress day might be announced unexpectedly. Cookies or cupcakes for everybody sometimes show up at lunch without prior notice. Surprise is an important facet of life; It keeps boredom at bay. It also provides an opportunity for a bit of mental stretching and a chance to think about how balance can actually be achieved in daily life.

Hanger Hall also actively uses exploration (See Chapter 9) to promote abstract reasoning. Some exploration is real, like engaging in role play, taking a short field trip, or traveling a bit more extensively. Other opportunities, however, involve imagination. The game "Now What?" (Chapter 9) teaches the girls to expect the unexpected and to mentally explore potential responses. Reflective learning (Chapter 10) also plays a role. The girls invent new endings for famous literary works or imagine how history might have changed under different circumstances. Cognitive skills like recognizing apparent dichotomies, thinking about how to achieve balance, and envisioning the range of life's possibilities are important. Like all other skills, performance improves with practice, and schools like Hanger Hall are in a perfect position to provide that practice.

What you think matters; but only if you really think it. - Rickie Lee, grade 7

Formal Operations: Reflecting on Multiple Perspectives

Young adolescents can also begin keeping track of several different viewpoints. During Concrete Operations, younger children learn that other perspectives exist. Now, those abilities are greatly enhanced. Simple recognition of multiple viewpoints is not enough. The fun comes in reflecting on why different outlooks make sense to different people.

The verb "reflect" comes from the Latin word *reflectere*, which means "to bend back." Bending back opinions and twisting around new ideas allow middle school girls to playfully practice their new-found cognitive skills. They can weigh the pros and cons of political platforms. They can compare and contrast the customs and practices of various religions. They can envision multiple solutions to a problem.

At Hanger Hall, the girls are asked to keep a travel journal for all trips. Time is allotted each day for the girls to take out their journals and make entries. The girls are encouraged to record anything and everything related to the trip and to their experiences on the trip. They are reminded often that this is their journal; and the teachers want this journal to reflect who they are and how they experience the trip.

Travel journals are not necessarily all prose or even all verbal. The girls are encouraged to try their hand at poetry or sketching. We encourage the girls to bring along colored pencils just for the purpose of illuminating their reflections. Then, at Group, each night, we invite (but never require) any of the girls to share from their journal.

Middle-school girls, whether they want to admit it or not, are also able to reflect on perspectives that differ from their own. They can understand why certain social skills are more important in some settings than in others. They can recognize that their parents, their friends, and the media will provide contradictory views on sexual activity. And they are increasingly aware of how events might be perceived by boys.

Formal Operations: Systematic Problem Solving

Even young children can solve problems. But, they are not particularly good at solving complex problems. They also tend to solve problems in a rather haphazard way. Let's say that you show children side-by-side pictures of two houses. The house on the left contains several windows with some sort of object (like a flowerpot or a curtain) in each one. The house on the right contains the same number of windows, also with an object in each one. The task is to determine whether or not the two houses are identical. If you watch the children's eye movements, younger children tend to move their eyes somewhat randomly. Their eyes wander around on the first house, wander around on the second house, and wander back and forth.

Older children, who are in Formal Operations, are much more systematic. Their eyes move from the top-left window of the left house to the top-left window of the right house, from the top-center window of the left house to the top-center window of the right house. In short, their problem-solving skills are significantly more orderly. Emerging adults also begin to solve problems somewhat scientifically – by holding one variable constant while testing all the others.

These cognitive skills can be readily applied to social situations. Hanger Hall recognizes that by utilizing something called "Group Challenge." It can happen in an individual classroom or when the entire school meets together. The Challenge can be presented by administration, faculty or student. A teacher might say, "I've noticed some cliques developing, and several girls are being excluded and getting their feelings hurt. The challenge is for you to help solve this problem." The challenge is then opened for discussion, allowing the girls to offer possible solutions. In the process, they get (and take) the opportunity to say why they "like to hang out more with certain girls." They also get to ask, "What's wrong with having best friends?" and "How can we still have best friends but include other girls?"

One time, four students made a formal request for help. They had been to a dance and music concert the previous weekend, which was performed by a group of children from an economically-depressed, clean-water-and-food-deprived country in Africa. The four students offered the challenge of finding ways to work with the children from this country to help them survive. The challenge got everyone involved with all kinds of "what-if's" and could we's?"

At other times, teachers may present challenges that deal with emotional issues, class projects, field trips, and behavior. Inevitably, teachers report that the students jump in with active discussion of ideas as to how these various matters of concern might be addressed. These open challenges empower the girls to take charge of the issues facing them, they demonstrate how a group of committed people can make a difference, and they often solve the problem in their own systematic way.

Rethinking Ages and Stages

Piaget's theory is still considered visionary by most developmental researchers; he literally transformed Western perceptions of childhood. Most parents and educators now view children as constructive learners who build on previous stages. We recognize that kids analyze vast amounts of incoming data to draw conclusions about the world around them. We even acknowledge that certain cognitive tasks are simply beyond the capabilities of younger children.

Collective thought advances, however, by moving beyond kudos, and Piaget's theory has been subject to widespread scrutiny. For the earlier stages, follow-up research from around the world has shown that Piaget often underestimated the age at which certain cognitive abilities emerge. Age estimates frequently decrease when researchers use objects that are highly familiar to the children. For example, children are able to adopt the perspective of another person at much younger ages when Sesame Street characters (rather than unfamiliar dolls) are used. Changing the wording of the instructions can also influence the results.

Other researchers have suggested that additional stages should be added to Piaget's original theory. Terms such as "pragmatic thinking," "dialectical thinking," "wisdom," and "problem-finding" have been coined to capture these cognitive advances that seem to emerge during adulthood. For example, adults may be better able to place their logical thinking in the context of real-world complexities. Solutions that make perfect sense at work may not make perfect sense at home. Public policy that works for a small town may be inappropriate for an entire state. For many theorists expanding abilities such as these deserve their own stage.

Despite such improvements, the fundamental descriptions that Piaget provided for the first three stages have held up reasonably well. Formal Operations, in contrast, has endured quite a bit of criticism. According to some researchers, less than half of American high school seniors would be placed in Formal Operations using Piaget's traditional measures. Thus, it is not clear that puberty always marks the onset of formal operational thinking. Even Piaget acknowledged that adolescents might be in their late teens before reaching this stage. Others have proposed that the college years might be a more accurate estimate. The actual use of formal operational strategies is also frequently inconsistent, regardless of age. People may have the ability to reflect on multiple perspectives or to solve problems systematically. Unfortunately, that doesn't mean they always make use of those abilities.

At least part of the explanation seems to revolve around specific life experiences. Formal operations are most likely to be used with highly familiar, culturally-relevant material. If the tribe demands high performance during hunting, then formal operations will frequently be applied under those circumstances. If the workplace routinely requires broken photocopiers to be fixed, then high-level cognitive strategies will appear in those situations. Explicit instruction also helps. Courses such as science and math promote systematic problem-solving. Academic disciplines such as history, literature, and art provide opportunities to reflect on multiple perspectives.

The implications for parents and teachers are nearly endless. New mental abilities open new avenues for thinking about how the world works. Schools should encourage discussion groups, debates, and problem-solving sessions. Families should swap ideas, trade perspectives, and exchange thoughts. Adolescents should be encouraged to think about their future and how to achieve their goals. They should be given a forum for addressing social concerns.

There are certainly other theoretical approaches. Some focus more on social development than cognitive development (See Chapter 5). Some provide an entirely new way to view cognitive development (Chapter 8). But Piaget was a first-rate intellectual of the 20th century. He shared his keen observational skills. He provided us with colorful descriptions. And he taught us that the cognitive journey to adulthood happens right before our very eyes – if we only take the time to notice.

Notes

1. Piaget wrote numerous books, both in French and in English. His work can be difficult to read, which is why many people read books written about Piagetian theory. If you would like to read something by Piaget himself, try Piaget, J. and Inhelder, B. (1969, 2000). *The Psychology of the Child*. NY: BasicBooks.

2. deVries, R. (1969). Constancy of generic identity in the years three to six. *Monographs of the Society for Research in Child Development*, 34(3).

Thinking About Thinking

Four
PURPOSE, GOALS & REFLECTION

I love thinking about thinking; but, it confuses me completely. - Ellen, grade 7

Continuing to develop and practice being an advocate for myself is one thing I really want to take away from Hanger Hall. I know I am academically prepared for high school. (I've watched my older brother go though high school with a lot easier homework load than I've had here.) But I also want to leave Hanger Hall taking away compassion and the ability to advocate –both for others and myself. That's how I think I'll leave my mark on the world around me in the next few years. - Marshall, grade 8

Q: Why do adults always ask children what they want to be when they grow up?
A: To get some ideas.

It's a standard question that kids get all the time: What do you want to be when you grow up? The question often comes when adults have run out of everything else to say: How old are you? What grade are you in? Do you play in any sports? Etc. And sometimes, children will have a pat answer: doctor, musician, basketball player. But, frequently, the answer is, "I don't know." Which, you must admit, sort of pinches off the conversation.

What the question is about, of course, is goals. We want goals for ourselves and we want our children to have goals. We want something to look forward to, something to work for, something to dream about, something to make plans for. Adults learn from life experience that, when you have a goal in mind, it can keep you motivated and excited when daily life becomes a grind. Whether you're looking forward to a vacation, a big concert, a visit from some favorite relative or even just looking forward to the weekend, simply having a goal keeps your engine in gear when the tendency otherwise might be to let it idle.

What's the Goal of Education?

Our entire educational system is based on goals. Grades are goals. Why do you study so hard and so many hours? So you can get a good grade. Why do you want to get a good grade? So you can get into a good college. Why do you want to get into a good college? So you can get a good job. Why do you want a good job? So you can do what you want to do and make more money. Etc. Indeed, this particular goal system has been called into question again and again.

We have, in many ways, equated the value of education to money. The formula has become: More education = More money. We continue to teach our children that the reason they're in school is to achieve more financial security. Rather than helping children see that learning is its own reward and dazzling the mind is a high and lofty goal, our society has reduced the goal and value of education to the bottom line - to the dollar.

One of our slogans at Hanger Hall is: Learning is not preparation for life; learning is life. We want our students to think of learning as life-long goal; and that learning, itself, is a reward. But, it's an uphill battle, because the message our girls hear through the media and through so much of society, is that learning is simply about making more money.

What our students hear is:
• Why do you stay in school? So you won't have to flip burgers the rest of your life.
• Why do you stay in school? So you can buy a new car.
• Why do you stay in school? So you can keep yourself in fancy clothes.
• Why do you stay in school? So you can retire comfortably.

And indeed, there are plenty of studies which show clearly that the longer you stay in school - high school, college, graduate school – the higher your career income will be. It's true. But, when the stated –or unstated - goal of education is nothing more than making a buck, we have lost something precious. We have lost a sense of wonder and delight in learning more about ourselves and world around us. We have lost an awareness of the values of a wizened mind and a scintillating wisdom which ask what life is about. If we are encouraging our middle school girls to set good goals for themselves, a good place to start is in education - to help these quickly maturing minds find delight in learning, to realize the intrinsic value of learning and to thereby set a goal for themselves to never stop learning.

Setting Life Goals

(After a science lesson demonstrating relative sizes of earth and sun: If sun is the size of a grapefruit, the earth is the size of a sesame seed): What's it all about anyway? The whole world to explore and who are we? Just tiny people on a sesame seed. – Olivia, grade 8

So, many times teachers and parents offer their children goals as rewards, or rewards for achieving goals:
• If you turn in your book report a day before the deadline, you'll get extra credit.
• When your room is cleaned up, we can rent that movie you want.
• If you bring home an "A" in history, you can have a party with your friends.
• If you give a report on amoeba that includes information not in the class science book, your letter grade goes up a notch.
• All A's this fall and you'll get an IPod. ….etc.

It is vital for middle school girls to see:
1) the value of setting goals,
2) the fun of working to achieve them,
3) the delight in celebrating when they are achieved and
4) the understanding that not all goals get met.
And one of the best ways to teach this goal-orientation is through example. Let's say you, as a parent, set a personal goal of losing ten pounds in two months. And,

instead of keeping that goal to yourself, you not only tell your middle-school daughter about your goal, you also enlist her help in achieving that goal. You ask her to remind you not to put too much on your plate, or to bypass that mid-afternoon soda, or to get out and do a power walk. When you ask your daughter to participate in achieving your own goals, you teach her not only the value of goals, but the goal-oriented process as well.

Teachers set goals for their students all the time. And, though most of these goals involve grades, grade point average and graduation, it is entirely possible to teach personal goal-setting as part of a class in study-skills and time management.

At Hanger Hall, personal organization is something we teach to every class, every year. We demonstrate how organizing your time can actually give you more time to do what you want; and we give our students tools to help them create and maintain that organization. Through this process, we encourage the students to set a goal for themselves to take control of their time and disallow the non-stop plethora of distractions to rob them of their time to 1) do what needs to be done; and 2) do what they want to do.

Middle school girls love the concept of taking control of their lives. It's a critical part of their social/emotional development. It is vital for these soon-to-be young women to know and experience the value of taking charge of their lives through time management, study skills and organization.

Compasses and Landmarks

In Chapter 3, we discussed Piaget's 4th Stage of development: Formal Operations. It is in this stage (middle-school age) that a child begins to think in abstract concepts. Theoretical perceptions. When a middle school girl enters the stage of formal operations, she enters the world of purpose. She has come, for perhaps the first time in her life, to the time when she can actually conceive not only of the concept of purpose, but what purpose she might develop for her life. It is one of the most exciting discoveries a girl or boy can make.

A younger child can talk and think about goals. Goals can be specific and defined. "Get yourself dressed," we tell a 6-year old; and the child knows immediately that getting dressed is the goal you have in mind. "Go get me three oranges," we tell an 8-year-old in the grocery store. And the 8-year-old should have no problem understanding and accomplishing that goal (although she may well come back with 3 oranges and a bag of candy.) But, it's not until the age of 10-12 for girls (and about 2 years later for boys) that the idea of purpose comes into play.

Goals can be realized or not. You can achieve your goal or fail at achieving it. It's very clear. But, the idea of purpose is different. Purpose is far more abstract than goals. Purpose is direction. Goals are the stops along the way.

Let's say your purpose is to make the front of your house look attractive and inviting. So, in order to fulfill your purpose, you might set some goals for yourself: mow the lawn, trim the shrubbery, paint the porch. Each of those goals is realizable. Each goal has a starting point and an ending. But, even after your goals are achieved – over and done with – your purpose is not finished. Your purpose remains intact: to make the front of the house look attractive and inviting. So, there might be other goals set and additional goals to go after. Have you achieved your purpose? Yes, in one sense; but that doesn't mean it's over and done with.

Purpose is a compass. Goals are landmarks. So, while your compass continues to point toward making your house attractive, your goals of mowing, trimming and painting come and go. (Of course, as we all know, the process of mowing, trimming and painting never really end. But when you finish one or the other, you can step back and say, "Aaahhh!")

A list of your personal purpose and goals might look like this:

PURPOSE	GOALS
Relax	Get a massage and take a hot bath
Vacation	Make hotel and plane reservations
Be more financially comfortable	Get a higher-paying job and save more
Lose weight	Eat less and move more
Be in a relationship	Get involved in civic or church groups
Be happy	(You fill in the blank)

A list for a middle school girl might be:

PURPOSE	GOALS
Be a good student	Study hard and regularly
Be a good daughter	Help out around the house and sort-of think about cleaning your room.
Look good	Buy clothes and fix hair
Have fun	Invite friends for a sleep over
Be happy	(She can fill it in)

Developmentally, your middle-school girl is capable of beginning to understand a theoretical concept like "purpose." And as her parent or teacher, you have a rare and golden opportunity to nurture that development and enable that young, budding adult to expand her awareness of the world and begin to visualize what her purpose(s) in this world might be and what goals she can set to follow and fulfill her purpose. You, as parent or teacher, have a literally once-in-a-lifetime chance to offer this amazing, emerging adult to see and begin to follow her soul's compass, and to focus on some viable landmarks.

Utilizing the Gift of Your Years

When it comes to purpose, you and your middle-schooler are probably a lot alike. It's highly plausible that both of you would share the life purposes of health, wealth and happiness. Not to mention success, fulfillment and lots of good times. But though your purposes are the same, your goals for achieving those purposes will inevitably be different in many ways. Happiness for you may not come by staying up all night with friends, listening to music, watching movies and talking about boys. Likewise, happiness will probably not bubble up inside your middle-schooler by going out to eat in a fancy restaurant with a bunch of drinking adults talking about golf games, the stock market and retirement plans. Goals may be different; but purposes are often shared.

The one singular, obvious and irreplaceable feature that distinguishes you as an adult and your middle-school girl, is life experience. You, as an adult, have been through so much more than she has. You have made so many more stupid choices and great decisions - glories and goofs - and have lived (and hopefully learned) through the joys and sorrows that followed. You have the gift of experience. Experience breeds perspective. Both good experience, and bad, generates perspective. And perspective can (not always, but) quite often lead to better judgment.

When it comes to defining purpose and following goals, your experience and resultant perspective can provide a matchless point of reference for your middle-schooler. She hasn't had enough years to realize, for example, that purpose doesn't get realized overnight; and sometimes it never get realized at all. She hasn't been around long enough to have failed in a variety of goals and to know that failure is part of the process of learning.

Nor has she lived long enough to have experienced so much of the delight which comes in achieving purpose or accomplishing goals. She, more than likely, hasn't had the chance to bask in the glory and rest in the comfort of that rich and full feeling which occurs when you sense that your life is on track and that you are living the life you are seeking to live.

Whether stated or unstated, one of the goals of most middle-school girls is to have friends. Most adults seek out and enjoy friends; but for middle-school girls, it's even more crucial. Vygotsky, the Russian author, teacher and psychologist, was quite clear that the social interactions between children and teachers or children and each other are absolutely critical in learning about themselves and the world around them. (See Chapter 8) Vygotsky was convinced that community provides not just social development, but cognitive development as well. So when a middle-school girl wants to have friends over, or go to a friend's house, she is actually providing for her developmental needs.

Likewise, when a middle-school girl is ditched or betrayed by a close friend, it can be devastating - devastating because of feeling hurt and rejected; and devastating because she may never have experienced this before and has no idea how a person can possibly live through it and ever be happy again.

You, as an adult, have, more than likely, had that experience. You have probably had it many times with friends, boyfriends, girlfriends, mates and even spouses. And with that irreplaceable life experience under your belt, you have the capacity to be with your middle-school girl, to hold her, and without even saying a word, offer a calm assurance that she will, indeed, be happy again. Because of your experience – the good, the bad and the ugly - you can offer your middle-schooler something she cannot offer herself. You can help her understand that, even though some things fall apart and purposeful goals get shot down, having purpose and chasing after goals is still a good thing.

Now, when life goes sour, you'll do yourself and your girl a favor if you keep in mind that you can't talk her out of her feelings. Yes, you've had life experience. And you can even share some of that experience with her. But remember: it's your experience. Not hers. You may have worked through yours in one way, but she's got to find her own way.

Trying to fix feelings is one of the biggest mistakes that adults make with children. Her feelings are her feelings; and they are vitally important. Her experience is her experience. Her life is her life. Though you can't talk her out of her feelings, you can be there for her and allow her to talk through her feelings. Life experience grants you the calm wisdom to do that. Life experience is not a magic wand; but life experience can provide a rock for her to lean on and cling to as she moves through her pain and prepares herself to follow the next part of her purpose.

And, if part of your purpose with that middle-school girl is to guide her on a course that will lead to self-confidence, one of the best goals you can have is the goal of being there for her when times are tough; and, with a gentle reassurance, helping her find her own words and ways to move through the hurt. Your life experience, combined with a healthy dose of compassion, can offer that middle-schooler one of the best tools she needs.

Working it Out
Clarity. Think clarity. Clarity is one of the greatest gifts you can offer a middle-school girl; and giving her the tools to find clarity will benefit her for the rest of her life. Keep in mind that the world of this emerging young woman is expanding exponentially by the moment. Her cognitive abilities are swelling and spreading into areas she had never known were there just a few years before. Her social development is sending emotional feelers and probes out into the world around her and deep within her. And, then, there's her body - growing and shifting in so many often confusing ways.

The universe of a middle-school girl can feel very muddled, jumbled and tangled, mixed-up, messed-up and cluttered like her room. In fact, some wise parents have suggested that messy rooms are simply a way of reflecting the mess that's inside. A cluttered room just might feel like home, especially if you feel cluttered inside. A messy room could be a reflection of what lies within, or it could be a working out of that messy emotional/mental/physical state. A messy room is a very concrete and visible expression, which just might be a way for a girl to get a handle on her inner workings.

On the other hand, there are middle-schoolers who are astoundingly neat. They make their beds, straighten their dressers and pick up their clothes even without a parental Genghis Khan demanding that the room be cleaned. And, it may well be that the neat and tidy or disastrously messy bedroom is one way for the middle-school girl to get a sense of clarity about what's going on inside her.

Confidence is courage. - Greta, grade 8

PAG's & PLG's

There are distinct ways that parents and teachers can help in this purpose/goal process. One way is by helping that middle-schooler make goals for her self. One of our instructors who teaches Time Management, Study Skills and Personal Organization, uses the acronyms: PAG for Personal Academic Goals and PLG for Personal Life Goals. This teacher contends that the first step in managing your time and organizing your daily life is to decide what you want to do with your time and what you want to do with your life. "If you're clueless about what direction you want to go," this teacher contends, "then you'll probably get there." In other words, plotting a course is an excellent way, she says, to get a handle on what you need to do and how you spend your day.

Plotting a course is a brilliant and easy way of helping your middle-school girl not only find some clarity, but actually create some clarity for herself. Writing down PAG's and PLG's is a clear and concrete way of actually plotting a course and making some sense out of the many demands being made on the student. Nor should the PAG and PLG lists be long. Five of each is plenty. Remember, the point of PAG's and PLG's – the point of time management, study skills and personal organization – is to make life easier, not more difficult. So, creating a long, impossible list of goals would be counter-productive.

Our teacher suggests that the students list their own PAG's and PLG's at the first of a school term. "You could have them make a list for the year," she says, "but that can be a bit overwhelming even for an adult." Then, she suggests that the initial list be placed somewhere that student will see it regularly - in the front of a notebook, on a mirror in her room, wherever...

Then, at the first of each week, the student makes a short list of PAG's and PLG's just for that week. Both the term list and the weekly list can be revised as the days pass and new opportunities and challenges appear. Creating and having the list is the important part. If the PAG's and PLG's are used properly, it gives the student a very real sense of control and direction. Nor is it wise to be overly anal about the lists. It is important to teach the student that some goals you achieve and some you don't. The point is to have some direction and to have some fun following that direction.

One PAG, of course, might be to "make a good grade." But, the students are encouraged to go deeper, asking questions like, "What kinds of things do I want to learn? What subjects intrigue me? What subjects do I want to get better at? What's out there in the world that I want to learn about? What smart people do I admire and want to emulate?"

Likewise, a PLG might be "to be happy and have a good time." But, here again, the students are encouraged to get into it a bit more, asking things like, "What kind of person do I want to be? What kinds of people and activities would help me be who I am? Could I learn to be a better friend? Could I find better friends? How can I improve my home life? My attitude? How can I keep from being bored?" Middle-school girls are fully capable of setting goals for themselves, and often thoroughly enjoy doing so. The process of setting goals offers the very-real awareness that they have some control over their lives; and this awareness is enormously vital in the development of self-confidence and self-assurance.

Our Time-Management teacher also reminds students to set PAG's for individual assignments. She suggests breaking up large projects into smaller chunks or separating material for big tests into smaller pieces. She suggests that the students set PAG's for each part of a project or test: times to work on each portion of the project or times to study each section of the test material. The teacher advises students to set self-deadlines for each part of the project or test – deadlines which are days (or even weeks) before the actual class deadline. "With these specific PAG's for specific class assignments," she says, "it makes the project seem far more doable; and no one holds you accountable but yourself." She also suggests that it's a good idea to reward yourself in some way when you achieve each of your PAG's.

Remember, with PAG's and PLG's, middle-school girls are beginning to think abstractly now. Encourage this. Girls this age are actively developing the mental facility to conceive of the concepts of learning, education, knowledge, culture and erudition along with the concepts of stupidity, dim-wittedness, ignorance, and unawareness.

Likewise, girls this age are daily becoming more and more capable of visualizing the ideas of beauty, wisdom, compassion, joy, excellence, wonder, delight, as well as pathos, repulsiveness, dull-mindedness, apathy, sorrow, mediocrity, ennui and anger. You will do your middle-schoolers a vast service in supporting their mental development by allowing them to think about and discuss these abstract perceptions in terms of their own PAG's and PLG's.

Making the World a Better Place
At Hanger Hall, Community Service is a vital part of our curriculum. Students are required to do two hours of community service each month during the school year.

Our definition of Community Service is threefold:
1) It must, in some way, make the world a better place.
2) There can be no money earned.
3) It can't be done for family.

The School provides at least one or two options for community service each month. The students can take advantage of those offering or find their own service opportunities.

The point of Community Service is also threefold:
1) To open up the students to the needs of the community;
2) To see that each of us can make a difference;
3) To understand "making the world a better place" as a valid purpose.

Middle-school girls are eager to discover worlds beyond their worlds. Yes, they want the comfort and ease of the known; but their constantly expanding cognitive and emotional potential is more than ready for new discoveries and fresh awareness. Community Service offers just that.

Constancy and Consistency

When a motion picture is being filmed, there is usually a person on the set who is in charge of continuity. It is this person's job to be sure that, as each take of each scene in the film is being shot, every effort is made to make sure that none of the props, clothing, hair, lighting or sound change; so that, when the scenes are all edited and assembled, it will appear absolutely seamless to the audience. It will appear to the viewer that a particular scene in the movie was filmed straight through from beginning to end, rather than being filmed at different times in smaller segments and then pieced together.

Moving through the middle-school years can give a girl the sense that things are broken up, disjointed and helter-skelter. Life can be that way for all of us, no matter how old we are. But, for the middle-schooler, all the vast variety of changes going on within and around her can be disorienting and unsettling. If there is one grand gift that you, as a parent or teacher, can give a middle-school girl, it is continuity. Constancy. Consistency. If she can have a sense that you are there – and will be there – for her, come what may, you will have offered her one of the most valuable contributions to her growth and development that anyone can give.

Creating PAG's, PLG's and opening up the concept of purpose to a middle-school girl are precious tools, indeed. For this young emerging woman to get the sense that she just might have a purpose in this life can go a long way toward helping her navigate the often tumultuous and confusing waters of the Sea of Pubescence.

But, as important as these tools may be, your continuity – your assuring presence that life goes on and that love and support real – can enable your middle-schooler to find her own footing and move in the direction her newly-found inner compass is pointing.

Reflection: Making it Real – Helping it Stick
Middle-school girls love to talk about themselves. And it's not from any narcissistic or egotistical emotional warps. Talking about your self, for a middle-school girl is one way of getting clearer about yourself. Talking about your self is a most excellent way of processing your ideas, behavior, feelings and opinions about whom or whatever. And becoming clearer about her self is exactly what a middle-school girl needs to be doing at this time in her life. Given that middle-school girls are daily becoming more and more able to grasp abstract concepts without concrete examples, discussions about individual purpose and goals can come naturally.

At Hanger Hall, we encourage the girls to journal about what they see, what they think, what they feel, what they hope for. We encourage them to write poems or draw pictures that express what's going on inside or around them. And in Group (See Chapters 1 and 5), we sometimes invite the girls to either share passages from their journals or talk openly about what's going on: on the inside and all around her. There is nothing like getting the cards on the table to help you see more clearly what you're holding in your hand, head or heart. That's what reflection is all about; and, in a properly relaxed environment, middle-school girls are both comfortable and eager to share their hopes and dreams, their failures and discouragements, their fears and joys.

Sometimes, when we're traveling with the girls, we will tell the girls that at evening Group, we'll devote 15 minutes to a subject like, "Exciting Dreams of the Future," or, "Fears About the Future;" or, maybe, "What I'm Really Good At and What I'm Not." When the girls get the word in advance and know that the discussion won't last forever, they are almost always eager to get the discussion started. And, many times, they want to go much longer than the allotted 15 minutes.

We have found that the best way to stimulate discussion – whether in groups or on a one-on-one basis – is genuine curiosity. Parenting author, Jane Nelson, points out that if you rearrange the letters of the word "listen," you get "silent." In other words, listening with honest-to-God curiosity is absolutely critical if you want your middle-school girl to offer some honest-to-God reflection. The listener must come with no agenda except to listen. Genuinely listen.

Does that mean that the listener must be completely silent? Of course not. That would be artificial and awkward for everybody. But, if you ask a group of middle-school girls about their hopes and dreams – and if you truly want them to express themselves – then, you'd better have an authentic interest in their hopes and dreams. Not just your hopes and dreams for them.

Reflection is one of the best ways to make this growing abstract concept of "purpose" real for your middle-school girl. And whether the reflection is vocal and shared, written in journal or letter, expressed in poem or prose or sculpture or paint or song, you can be sure that reflection can help provide both clarity and glue, understanding and coherence. Offering your emerging woman the chance to explore her inner compass and landmarks is one incredible gift to her development as a strong and self-directed woman.

Why bother with the harbors when there's an ocean? - Grace, grade 7

- *Five* -
THE SOCIAL SCENE

Friends here (Hanger Hall) are great. You never have to feel like you can't be yourself.
- Stella, grade 7

Who Am I?

Ask a child "who are you?" and you will get some fairly simple answers. "I'm Sarah!" "I'm a kid!" "I'm a second-grader." Ask an adult and you will get a different set of responses. "I'm a dad." "I'm a teacher." "I'm a Catholic." "I'm a Republican." Such statements provide a glimpse into our identity – how we live, who we live with, what we believe, what we do. But how do we move from "I'm a girl" to "I'm a pacifist"? Psychologists would probably recommend starting with Erik Erikson (1902-1994).

Erikson and Personality Development

Erikson was trained as a psychoanalyst at the Vienna Psychoanalytical Institute, graduating in 1933.[1] He also studied the Montessori method of education.[2] By combining his educational background with his skilled observations of children and families, Erikson put forth a stage theory that follows the same general guidelines as Piaget's stage theory. Erikson's theory, however, focuses more specifically on personality development. His theory also contains eight stages (rather than Piaget's four), and unlike Piaget, several of his stages happen during adulthood.

Erikson describes each stage as a social conflict that must be resolved. For example, the first stage, which roughly corresponds to the first two years of life, is called Trust vs. Mistrust. During this stage, infants must determine whether or not the world is a caring place where they will be fed, clothed, and comforted. The hope is that the conflict will be resolved positively as opposed to negatively. If so, infants will learn security and optimism. That knowledge will then serve as the foundation for other challenges to come. As you might suppose, Erikson's social conflicts get mighty interesting during the adolescent years.

As a parent, I often remind myself of Erikson's theory when I'm dealing with seemingly annoying behaviors from my children. "Why does it take so long for my three-year-old to get into her car seat?" I wondered. It's not a particularly difficult task. And, by law, it happens every single time she gets into the car. "Is it really necessary for her to pick up that stale, sticky candy wrapper off the floor of the backseat?" I ask myself. "Is it really necessary to push all the window and door lock buttons? They don't even work until the car is turned on." And then Erikson's stages flash before me.

Toddlers are learning autonomy and independence (instead of trust and mistrust). When three-year-olds do what they want, when they want, they are exercising their newfound toddler identities. They are individuals who are discovering their own desires; and they have the growing capacity to achieve them. In developing a family community, everyone's needs must alternate between the forefront and the background. The errands must be run, and parents are frequently in a hurry. But sometimes it's beneficial to recognize the joys of development – even if it means letting your five-year-old get distracted by a colorful bug. Just remember, in Erikson's world, you're promoting curiosity and wonder (instead of boredom and indifference).

Industry and Inferiority

The middle two stages (4 and 5) in Erikson's theory are the most important for middle-school girls. Stage four, called Industry vs. Inferiority, corresponds to the grade school years. On the positive side, children learn that hard work pays off, and they feel pride in their accomplishments. On the negative side, children learn that there is little relationship between effort and reward, and they sometimes feel ashamed of their attempts. Girls entering middle school are nearing the end of this stage. For girls moving toward successful resolution of this stage, Hanger Hall provides ways to reinforce those social gains. A positive transition to middle school is facilitated by the school's efforts to build community (See Chapter 1), to use clear-cut behavioral guidelines (Chapter 2), to offer advising time (Chapter 7) and to expect solid academic effort (Chapter 10). For girls who are leaning toward negative resolution, these same opportunities offer a way to revise, redefine, or even reverse the current trend.

We all live in a yellow submarine. - Stella, grade 7

Identity and Role Confusion

Erikson called stage 5 Identity vs. Role Confusion. Erikson clearly understood that identity development is a lifelong process, but he also recognized that identity formation is the fundamental social challenge of the adolescent years. In Piaget's theory, the transition to puberty marked an important shift in thinking ability. In Erikson's theory, the transition marks an important shift in the social realm. For girls, once again, middle school provides the setting. You can probably guess that establishing a strong personal identity and a sense of fit in the social world represents the healthy developmental path. Decisions must be made about relationships, careers, and value systems. The groundwork must be laid for a functional adult life.

But how does this happen? Erikson intentionally chose the term "crisis" to describe this process.[3] More recent theorists often use terms like "exploration" or "experimentation." The underlying concept, however, remains the same: Young people try on new selves. They dress in non-conforming ways. They associate with atypical groups of friends. They engage in new types of relationships, some of them intimate. They explore other religious traditions. They join various clubs. They investigate alternate political points of view. When you cringe as your pink ballerina morphs into a goth rocker, or when you recoil at the thought of your football-playing tomboy buying designer clothes at the mall, it might help to remind yourself

- ever so briefly - of Erikson. Those bewildering behaviors are helping your changeling to establish a sense of self.

Ultimately, choices are made and an identity is formed. But these decisions are rarely finalized during middle school. Instead, middle school provides the stage for the opening scenes. Middle-school girls begin noticing the range of possibilities that life offers. They contemplate the world around them and try to imagine their place in it. They assess their own abilities and interests and try to match them to real-world opportunities.

Hanger Hall promotes identity formation in countless ways. For example, at their 8th grade graduation, each girl makes a two-minute speech to the assembled students, faculty, administration, parents, grandparents, and goofy relatives. They begin working on this speech in the spring, finish it up a month before graduation and then practice it. Each year, the theme for the speech varies a bit, but we always ask the girls to address three questions. What have I discovered about myself while at Hanger Hall? How has Hanger Hall helped me become who I am? Given who I am, how can I help make the world a better place? It is fascinating to hear these girls talk about ideas, impressions, and possibilities. Talk about intangible and theoretical notions all centered on their own awareness of themselves.

Hanger Hall also expands horizons through ritual (See Chapter 1) and travel (Chapters 6 and 9). The teachers ask, in all sorts of wild and wonderful ways, about the hearts and minds of the students (Chapter 6). They actively, and explicitly, teach social skills (Chapter 7). They incorporate silliness and humor. In short, they understand that one of the biggest tasks a middle schooler must accomplish is finding her place in the world.

Who knows where identity development will lead? Some people eventually develop an identity that is quite different from their upbringing. Others explore but return to their familial roots. Either way, at Hanger Hall, they understand that one of biggest tasks a middle schooler must accomplish is developing a sense of self and finding her place in the world. The two go hand in hand. Developing a sense of self helps you find your place. Finding your place helps you develop a sense of who you are. Picture them dancing together. Sometimes one leads, sometimes the other. The music and beat to which they are dancing comes from the world around them. The goal for the teachers and parents of middle-schoolers remains the same as for any other developmental period – to appreciate the dance.

A Brief History of Self Esteem

In the early 1990s, there was mounting evidence that girls were forming their identities in a negative context. During adolescence, rates of depression increase. The likelihood of experiencing an eating disorder soars. Family conflict intensifies. Adolescent girls appeared to be drowning with no lifeboat in sight. Concern was heightened by the work of Carol Gilligan,[4] the American Association for University Women,[5] Peggy Orenstein,[6] and Mary Pipher,[7] all of whom offered compelling indications that girls risk losing their way during middle school and high school.

Gilligan's early work actually focused on the development of moral judgment. Her research technique, which had been used by others,[8] involved the presentation of moral dilemmas to children of different ages. Moral dilemmas basically involve placing an individual between two difficult moral choices – like letting a family member die in order to save several other people or exposing the confidential information of one person in order to help someone else.

Like Piaget, Gilligan was somewhat unconcerned about whether an answer was "right" or "wrong." Instead, she wanted to know how children explained their answers. Her conclusion was that boys adopt more of a justice perspective. They are concerned with equality and fairness, and those are the standards they use to make moral decisions. Girls, in contrast, adopt more of a care perspective. They focus on relationships and community interactions when making moral decisions. According to Gilligan, the problem arises when girls begin to realize that the care perspective is less valued in American society. They become insecure about their opinions and are less likely to express their ideas. They "lose their voice."

Orenstein came to a similar conclusion in her best-seller *Schoolgirls: Young Women, Self-Esteem and the Confidence Gap*. Orenstein spent an entire school year interacting with eighth-grade girls in two California middle schools. Using her journalism skills, she interviewed the girls, as well as their parents and teachers. She also attended classes, visited homes, and observed the girls during their extracurricular activities.

She concluded that the school environment often lowers the self-confidence of girls. The standard school curriculum is often male-centered, and the hidden curriculum[9] often perpetuates myths about gender-appropriate behavior. Broader American culture tends to value personality traits like independence, assertiveness, and risk-taking, which are typically associated with men. This same culture tends to devalue personality traits like sensitivity, patience, and helpfulness, which are typically associated with women. The end-product is a confidence gap between the genders with girls feeling significantly less confident than boys. As a result, girls are more likely to perform poorly in school, to participate in unhealthy sexual behavior, or to seek out gang-related activity.

This overall view was further supported by Pipher in her best-seller *Reviving Ophelia: Saving the Selves of Adolescent Girls.* As a therapist, Pipher used case studies to underscore the social problems unique to adolescent girls. In her view, adolescent girls in America don't just lose their voice, or their self-confidence, they lose their selves:

Girls' symptoms reflect the grief at the loss of their true selves. Their symptoms reflect the confusion about how to be human and be a woman. The basic issues appear and reappear in many guises. Girls must find, define and maintain their true selves. They must find a balance between being true to themselves and being kind and polite to others. Pathology often arises in girls because of the failure to realize their true possibilities of existence… (p.259)

Where Are We Now?

Has anything changed since the early 1990s? Are adolescent girls really that bad off? Are all girls destined to experience a significant life crisis during adolescence? Are girls really worse off than boys? The answer to all of these questions is yes – and no. Research findings published in the late 90s and early 2000s have brought some clarification. This increased knowledge provides important clues for parents and teachers trying to help middle-school girls successfully navigate their increasingly complex social world.

First, even mediocre observers can see that individuals move through adolescence differently, and the research bears this out. At least some girls enter middle school with a high level of self-esteem, and their self-esteem stays high. Other girls actually show an increase in self-esteem during the middle-school and early high-school years. African Americans, on average, tend to have higher self-esteem than other ethnic groups. White Americans tend to come next. Girls from supportive families that communicate productively are more likely to have high self-esteem. Encouragement from other significant adults, like teachers or coaches, can also enhance self-esteem. Such findings clearly suggest that low self-esteem during the middle school years is not pre-destined. Families, schools, and other institutions all have a potential role to play, and Hanger Hall takes this role seriously.

Second, most researchers now believe that self-esteem encompasses several factors, including scholastic aptitude, athletic skill, social ability, and physical attractiveness. Thus, a girl could have high self-esteem in one area, like artistic performance, but low self-esteem in another area, like competence in developing friendships. Overall self-esteem depends on which factors are most important to the individual girl. Some girls are not particularly athletic, but they don't really care. Some girls have few friends and are happy that way (See Chapter 9 – Loners). Regardless of individual differences, there may be some general trends. School success is often highly related to self-esteem. (This is especially true for Asian Americans.) Physical attractiveness is also an important factor for most adolescent girls (but ethnic differences have been reported on that variable as well). Taken together, then, the current assumption is that self-esteem isn't quite as simple as we used to think. Self esteem is made up of several components. Moreover, the relative value of those components depends on the individual, the family, and the culture.

Being complex, however, is not equivalent to being unmanageable. Global self-esteem is most likely to decline during adolescence, but assuming that all middle-school girls are experiencing the same struggles to the same extent is somewhat off the mark. Each girl experiences her own version of adolescence. Optimal nurturing therefore requires an individualized approach. What aspects of self-esteem are most likely to be affected in a particular child? How can self-esteem be maintained or increased in specific life areas? What matters most to that budding woman standing in front of you? The only way to really answer those questions is to pay attention. To ask. To listen. To watch. To care.

The good news is that self-esteem can be enhanced through praise and affirming self-talk. Explicitly remind children of their positive attributes. Encourage them to focus on their strengths. Help them to recognize and value their accomplishments. Provide perspective. On those days when nothing seems to be working, it might make sense to just hang on for the ride. The really good news is that self esteem is quite likely to rise again during adulthood.

Self-Consciousness and Emotionality

Despite the mounds of research and media attention heaped on self-esteem, the term itself may simply represent a modern way of expressing a very old notion. Adolescent angst and teenage turmoil have served as fodder for movies, books, poems, and love songs for centuries. Both Socrates (470BC-399BC) and Aristotle (384BC-322BC) commented on the turbulence of adolescence. European writers in the 1700s penned stories about the impulsive nature of puberty. And psychologists in the early 1900s waxed eloquent on the "storm and stress" model of adolescent development.

Modern-day researchers focus on self-consciousness and emotionality – probably with good reason. The evidence suggests that both self-consciousness and emotionality intensify during the adolescent years. Moreover, both factors are inversely related to self-esteem. As self-consciousness goes up, self-esteem goes down. As emotionality increases, self-esteem decreases.

Overall, adolescents do appear to be less happy than younger children. Adolescents say that they feel self-conscious, awkward, and embarrassed significantly more often. They are less likely to say that they feel happy or proud at any given time. They are more likely to say that they feel sad or lonely. Adolescent emotions also appear to be less stable. When compared to adults, adolescents are more likely to say that they feel "very happy" and more likely to say that they feel "very sad." This emotional roller coaster, which may be more widespread for girls compared to boys, maddens parents and frustrates teachers.

At least some of the feelings probably stem from the new mental abilities that emerge during puberty. As Piaget described (See Chapter 3), middle-school girls are learning to think abstractly and to reflect on multiple perspectives. They are now cognitively able to mull over their own lives and ruminate on the views of others. One result of these thought processes is the creation of, and the near obsession with, "an imaginary audience."[10] We've all experienced the imaginary audience. This audience notices every flaw, every blemish, and every imperfection. The audience members sit around all day and ponder the small pimple on your nose, the miniscule scratch on your neck, and the single, out-of-place hair. For this audience, you are the show, and the play moves deftly from tragedy to comedy and back to tragedy again in a matter of hours.

Both younger children and older adults experience some version of an imaginary audience. It allows us to feel pride and embarrassment. It ensures that we comb our hair and brush our teeth every morning. It provides the cultural mirror that facilitates self-reflection. But this imaginary audience tends to be much more prominent, much more critical, and much more significant during adolescence. It also becomes much more peer-oriented. Kids can be the harshest critics. When they are assembled in your head as a jeering posse, watching every tiny developmental misstep, feelings of awkwardness skyrocket.

As with self-esteem, however, the findings on self-consciousness and emotionality tend to highlight general trends. Numerous factors influence the extent to which changes are actually observed in any given child. Family dynamics, ethnic group, the presence of life stressors, and the manner in which life events are interpreted all play a role. Multifaceted? You bet. Incomprehensible? Not really.

Even if the research can't guarantee that reducing awkward feelings will enhance self-esteem, it sure provides ideas for trying. Every effort should be made to communicate effectively and respectfully, even when it feels frustrating and unproductive. Parents should provide a caring, adult perspective, even when it seems to be rejected or unappreciated. Schools should also lend a helping hand, even when they would rather avoid responsibility. Hanger Hall demonstrates various ways to reduce the negative feelings associated with middle school – developing a sense of community (See Chapter 1), offering care and compassion (Chapter 2), asking/listening (Chapter 6), and explicitly teaching social skills (Chapter 7). There are no sure bets here, but you can certainly boost your odds.

Pin the Tail on the Culprit

While some investigators continue to sort out the relationships between self-consciousness, emotionality, and self-esteem, other researchers focus on the underlying, driving forces. The most obvious changes that occur during puberty are physical. Since most readers are probably on the far side of puberty, I won't review the details here. If your memory is failing, or if you simply wish to relive the events, try an internet search on the term "puberty." You should end up with over 10 million sites to choose from, including some questionable on-line videos. Yes, there are some changes that are less visible – like enlargement of the ovaries and changes to the vaginal mucosa – but most of us have the general idea.

Of greater interest, perhaps, is that an equally transformative process may be taking place in the brain. Caregivers, educators, media staffers, and government workers have all been intrigued by several sets of recent research findings. Investigations continue, but a fascinating picture is already beginning to materialize.

First, the cells of the brain – neurons – become more effective in communicating with one another during development. Neurons are often partly covered with fatty tissue, called myelin, that functions much like the insulation on an electrical wire. It allows the brain's electrical impulses to be delivered more quickly from one neuron to the next.

We now know that the myelination process continues throughout the teen years, and it continues in several parts of the brain. Neurons that connect one lobe of the brain to another show increases in myelin. The corpus callosum, a bundle of fibers that connects the left and right hemispheres, thickens with myelin. And many neurons that make connections within a lobe, especially those of the frontal lobe (behind the eyes) also gain myelin. The basic neuron-to-neuron connections are present at birth, but the myelin changes strongly suggest that information is now being transmitted more quickly and more effectively.

Second, the brain begins to select which connections it will keep. Throughout childhood, the brain produces more neurons than it needs, and those neurons have more processes than necessary. It might seem as though more is better. However, the brain uses large amounts of energy to fuel neurons. It has been estimated that the brain consumes about 10 times as much energy as the rest of the body combined, which means there is a cost to having lots of neurons sitting around. This is especially true if particular neurons and their associated processes are not being used much.

During adolescence and early adulthood, the brain engages in "pruning," a withering away of extra neurons and superfluous connections. Cellular pathways that are used remain. Cellular pathways that are unused die off. Some researchers have estimated that the brain may lose between 7-10% of its cortex between the ages of 12 and 20. While this process may seem tragic, it actually allows the brain to communicate more efficiently. It also happens in important brain areas, like the prefrontal cortex and the cerebellum. The prefrontal cortex is found at the very front of the front part of the brain. It is involved in planning and decision-making. The cerebellum is located in the lower, back part of the brain. It is involved in complex learning and social skills.

Third, chemical levels in the brain also change during this time. Neurons contain chemicals, called neurotransmitters, which are used in cell-to-cell communication. If neurons and their processes are reorganizing, then the chemical make-up of the brain is bound to change as well. Particular attention has been paid to dopamine and serotonin levels in the limbic system. The limbic system (See Chapter 6) is a series of structures deep in the brain known to be involved in memory, emotions, and sexuality. Dopamine and serotonin are important brain chemicals known to be involved in movement, sleep, depression, and rewards.

When you put all these bits of information together, you begin to get a sense of how emotional state might be altered during puberty. Neurons containing dopamine and serotonin are being myelinated and pruned. As a result, neurotransmitter levels are increasing in some regions and decreasing in others. Since some of those regions are directly tied to social/emotional functioning, we would expect to see visible changes in behavior. And many times, we do.

The potential relationship between all of these brain changes is also fascinating. Limbic system changes, which presumably affect emotion, probably happen during puberty, which is most likely to occur during middle school for girls. Changes in the prefrontal cortex, however, are not complete until the mid-20s. Thus, the emotional parts of the brain reach adult-like status before the reasoning parts of the brain. The emotions are there – in full force – but the ability to manage them is not. A similar story may hold for the cerebellum. "Storm and stress" has been associated with adolescence for centuries, but we're only now beginning to discover how the unevenness of neural development might play a role.

Ch…Ch…Ch…Changes

During middle school, a girl's physical, cognitive, and social world undergoes an enormous shift. The extraordinary changes can eat away at confidence, self-reliance, and identity. Or, they can serve as a jumping-off point for the creation of a strong, resilient sense of self. There may be little to be done about hormonal increases and brain development during puberty. The research findings on self-esteem, self-consciousness, and emotionality may be overwhelming or flat-out annoying. And decisions about the self are ultimately personal and private. However, no developmental outcome is entirely pre-determined. There are options as well as opportunities. Family members, friends, teachers, and mentors should help out. So go ahead and throw in your two cents on occasion. Just try to do it in a positive and understanding way, even if the response you get is not.

Notes

1. The Institute grew out of the Vienna Psychoanalytical Society, which was founded by Sigmund Freud and his followers in the early 1900s. Freudian psychoanalyzes is centered on early childhood experiences, which were thought have significant effects on adult personality. He also placed a great deal of emphasis on unconscious conflict, much of which was sexual. Freud's followers often retained certain components of his theory (unconscious conflict, for example), while eliminating others (an extreme focus on sexual issues).

2. The Montessori method of education is based on the work of Italian educator Maria

Montessori (1870-1952). Like Piaget, she believed that children view the world differently than adults. Thus, they have different educational needs. Montessori learning is hands-on and self-directed, with children taking a significant lead in what they learn. The teacher is a guide rather than a lecturer. Little to no emphasis is placed on traditional measures of academic success, like tests and grades.

3. The term "crisis" stems from the concept of unconscious conflict that is fundamental to Freud's psychoanalytical theory. Such conflict must be resolved to alleviate anxiety and end the crisis.

4. Gilligan, C. (1982). *In a Different Voice: Psychological Theory and Women's Development*. Cambridge, MA: Harvard University Press.

5. American Association of University Women (1992). *How Schools Shortchange Girls: The AAUW Report: Executive Summary*. Washington DC: AAUW. Also, American Association of University Women (1995). *How Schools Shortchange Girls: The AAUW Report: A Study of Major Findings on Girls and Education*. New York: Marlowe and Company.

6. Orenstein, P. (1994). *Schoolgirls: Young Women, Self-Esteem, and the Confidence Gap*. New York: Anchor Books.

7. Pipher, M. (1994). *Reviving Ophelia: Saving the Selves of Adolescent Girls*. New York: Riverhead Books.

8. The use of moral dilemmas to assess moral decision-making is most commonly associated with Lawrence Kohlberg. On the basis of his research with males, he proposed three levels of moral development (preconventional, conventional, postconventional), with each level containing two stages. Follow-up studies suggested that girls operated at a lower level than boys, a controversial finding that Gilligan attempted to address.

9. The term "hidden curriculum" refers to the idea that schools do more than teach content. They also transmit information about social policy (through rules and other means of social control), about political structures (usually with a focus on democracy), and about the broader culture. Many sources argue that the hidden curriculum is real, even though it may be unintended.

10. Elkind, D. (1967). Egocentrism in Adolescence. Child Development, 38, 1025-1034.

- *Six* -
DEALING WITH FEELINGS

At Hanger Hall all the teachers are easy to talk to. They can tell if you're having a bad day or need someone to talk to. Hanger Hall is a very comfortable place to be and always welcoming. I like it because everywhere I go I'm treated with a smile
- 8th grader

Blame it on the Amygdala

The amygdala is an almond-shaped neuro structure located within the temporal lobes of the brain. It lies close to the hippocampus and is in a direct line with the hypothalamus. Its size varies from human to human. Some studies have found that it is enlarged in those suffering from depression and smaller in those addicted to cocaine. But overall, for the average human, the amygdala is less than one centimeter across, about the size of an almond. In fact, amygdala is actually the word for "almond" in Latin.

Such a tiny little part of the brain; and yet, that little almond packs a punch. When you're angry, for example, and shake your fist or glare at someone, it's probably your amygdala doing its thing. Likewise, if you are walking down a dark street, hear a strange noise, suddenly feel afraid and, without thinking begin to run once again, the involuntary running is probably prompted by that almond in your head.

When you're feeling anxious or uncomfortable for one reason or another, your amygdala can trigger unconscious body movements or facial expressions. It can trigger sweaty palms and gritting teeth. Your brain almond is what causes shoulder and neck muscles to tense and thereby keeps massages therapists employed. It also prompts the release of adrenaline and kicks in the fight or flight syndrome.

One Brain – Three Parts

One theory of how the brain works, proposed in the 1950's by Paul McLean, faculty member Yale Medical School, theorizes a three part brain: 1) The brainstem – or so-called "reptilian brain" or "R-Complex," 2) the limbic system and 3) the neo-cortex. The reptilian brain is the portion of your gray matter, which you, all humans and all mammals share with reptiles. You share this part of your brain with snakes and alligators, lizards and turtles. This is the portion of the brain responsible for survival behavior, including extreme anger and fear of the unknown.

Parts of this reptilian brain can be triggered into action by the limbic system (also called the mammalian brain). The amygdala and hippocampus are part of that limbic system. The limbic system, according to McLean, is also the source of some parts of personal identity and is, therefore, vital to the middle-school girl.

According to Dr. McLean, the third part of the brain is the neo-cortex, which is found in the more recent mammals to appear on earth (including you and every other human). The neo-cortex is the portion of the brain which offers the possibility of reason, speech, culture art and literature. Unfortunately, not all humans take full advantage of our neo-cortex. A good teacher and parent can help with that.

Here Come the Hormones

But, what makes the amygdala, hippocampus and the rest of the limbic system important to teachers and parents of middle-school girls is this: it's where hormones come from. The dreaded hormones. Have a conversation with any parents or teachers of middle-schoolers and, chances are, that within the first few minutes of conversation, you'll hear the word, "hormones." Hormones are blamed for almost everything in middle-school behavior; but, particularly, hormones are blamed for heightened sexual awareness and activity.

And the blame is well-deserved. But, hormones have a far greater role in pubescent development than simply the activation of the reproductive parts. So what is a hormone? Think of a hormone as a biological cell phone. In fact, hormones are, indeed, "cell" phones. Hormones enable cells to communicate. Chemical messengers they are, carrying messages from one cell to another. Now, keep in mind that many of these cells in your middle-school girl have lived side-by-side for 9-10-11 years, and have never communicated. It's not a matter of animosity or any ill feeling between the cells. These cells sitting right up close and personal for years simply haven't been in touch with each other. Once hormones show up, however, these cells can begin chatting; and once that begins to happen, all kinds of expansive changes begin to occur.

OK, It's Not all Amygdala's Fault

Now, the amygdala may be one of the producers of hormones; but it is the hypothalamus which oversees all the hormonal activity. It is the hypothalamus which coordinates blood pressure, body temperature and immune responses. It affects your sense of thirst and hunger and can actually control your food intake. It regulates your panting and sweating when your body temperature rises. It triggers growth, stimulates a wide variety of emotional behavior (can you say, "mood swings?"), stimulates sexual activity and manages Circadian rhythms (when and how much we sleep, for example).

In short, the hypothalamus directs, stimulates and coordinates the way we feel. The way we feel at any given moment. So, perhaps, we shouldn't blame it all on the amygdala. Maybe it's all in the hypothalamus' court.

The point here is that you can't blame your middle-schooler's mood swings, sleep cycles, sexual giddiness or eating patterns on any one thing. Your middle-schooler (like yourself) is an amazing and complex organism within which are many, many parts – each communicating and affecting the other parts. Hormones make that communication possible. And, it is when this cellular communication kicks into high gear (almost always between the ages of 10-15) - when the cells of the body begin to interact with each other in earnest - that all manner of growth starts happening: physical growth, emotional growth, cognitive growth and social growth. It is during this critical time – this precious window of time – that your middle-school girl is expanding and developing in absolutely every way. It is during these irreplaceable years that she has the once-in-a-lifetime opportunity to develop and become everything her DNA is calling her to be. Every possibility, every talent and gift dancing in her chromosomes has the chance during this time to begin its journey and to define the uniqueness of this emerging young woman. During these decisive years, that middle-school girl has extraordinary chance to discover for herself who she is and what she might be and become in this world.

Feelings… Whoa-Whoa-Whoa, Feelings

Even with a fair overview of what is biologically happening inside your middle-school girl, it can still be an enormous challenge for parents and teachers to deal with all the feelings, emotions, moods, interests, sleep-cycle-changes, sexual awareness, thoughts, demonstrative separation from family, active rebellion, passive/aggressive behavior and on and on.

Parents and teachers must constantly keep in mind, that, like a chick emerging from a shell… like a baby emerging from a mother's womb… like a butterfly emerging from a chrysalis, a middle-school girl is emerging from 10 years of childhood into young adulthood; and, like every other new life, it can be messy. It can be very messy. And, for the parent and teacher, simply coming to accept that messiness as part of the process can go a long way toward 1) easing the parent's and teacher's minds, and 2) giving the young emerging adult the grace and space to move through these enormous changes.

What Works?

Just as there is no clear pattern of growth that happens right on schedule with each and every middle-school girl, there is, likewise, no clear answer as to what always works with each and every parent or teacher in dealing with middle-schoolers' feelings. We can remind ourselves till the cows come home that this tidal wave of feelings from our middle-schoolers is the result of necessary growth; but, 1) the emotional upheaval can be tremendously nerve-wracking and stressful for everybody; and 2) it is important – no, it is absolutely vital – that middle-schoolers have some competent adult or adults to be with them as they move through this incredibly significant growth phase in their lives.

As a parent of two young women who are now on the adult side of pubescence, and as an educator who has worked in schools for 30 years and has served as Founder and Headmaster of an all-girls' middle school, I have learned a few things. Although, I must say that almost every time I speak with another educator or parent of one of these amazing beings, I learn something new. And one of the most important things I have learned is that what works well on one day may not work at all the next day. And what works well with one middle-schooler may not be worth a diddle to another.

Be that as it may, when it comes to dealing with feelings, there are two basic and oh-so-simple precepts by which we operate at Hanger Hall School. We have found these fundamental principles to help our students move through their astounding and tumultuous years. And, though we would certainly never claim that this modus operandi as the be-all and the end-all, we – as faculty and administration – have found that these basic principles are finally effective in providing the soil and nurture for these young, pubescent seedlings to grow into healthy blooming adults. And what are these magical guidelines? They are simply, ask and listen.

Keep in mind, however, that asking and listening are based on the premise that we care about these kids. Without an active and genuine concern for these girls, anything we do is not only hollow, but also hypocritical. One thing is certain: Middle-school girls have feelers a mile long. Their intuition is frighteningly exceptional. They can pick up on insincerity and pretense faster than a politician can practice it. So, if you truly don't truly care about what happens to the middle-schooler who is in your charge, best that you go do something else. They will know. They will, most certainly, know.

And there are two more little items: 1) The following asking/listening guides are not meant to be used just when things get crazy with your middle-schooler. On the contrary, asking and listening is best employed when things are not crazy. Then, when things do get crazy, the asking and listening is ever so much more meaningful. 2) When you're asking and listening, be real. Be yourself. Remember the feelers. Authenticity is absolutely vital.

Everyone here (Hanger Hall) is your friend. Even the teachers. You can tell them anything. - Lucy, grade 7

The Guidelines: Ask & Listen
A) Ask
Everyone has the need to feel important in some way - uniquely important. We each-and-all have the desire to feel as if who we are and what we think are significant. So, simply asking the question, "How's it going?" can do a lot. If you're familiar with middle-schoolers, of course, you can almost always count on the response to the question being mono-syllabic, as in, "Fine," or "Good," or "Bored."

If that's all you get, don't be daunted. You've opened the door. Try another, "What have you been doing lately? Having any fun?" And so on. You get the picture. The point is to show interest. Honest-to-God-no-strings-attached-no-hidden-agenda interest. The point is for you to actually get to know a bit about what's going on in this utterly unique life that is there in front of you.

Ask Real Questions
The truth of it is that, when you ask real questions which are rooted in genuine interest, you will get real answers. You may not get the answers you want; but you'll get real answers, indeed. You will learn things about this young girl; and more than likely, you will learn things about yourself and of the world around you. Middle-schoolers are riding the cusp between child and adulthood. It's a cusp that we ride only once in this life. And the perspective from that cusp can be eye-opening.

Mind-expanding. The perspective from that cusp can, indeed, provide insight into what's going on in your own life.

Depending on how well you know the girl and how much history you have with her, you can ask about her family, her friends, her activities, her favorite movies, favorite food, music, video game, sport, pet, vacation, subject in school, favorite teacher (unless, of course, you are her teacher). The point of asking questions is to 1) get to know this amazingly unique girl and to 2) help her get to know herself and begin realize just how amazingly unique she is.

If you sense that it's OK, you can even ask about her feelings. "What's the happiest thing you've done lately?" or "Has it been a happy week for you?" Middle-school girls – if they are comfortable - like to talk about themselves. They may not talk long; but simply opening that door can work wonders for both of you.

Asking questions seems so simple and primitive. You might wonder, "Where are the sophisticated academic/psychological tools and methods to deal with these kids? What's with this mundane question and answer business?" And well you might ask. But sometimes we forget that humans have been going through pubescence for as long as we've been riding this planet. This is nothing new. Moving through this time of life is not brain surgery; it is brain expansion. And it is precisely the simplicity of making genuine adult/emerging-adult connections that can bring that marvelous and miraculous expansion to light and open even more doors of self-discovery.

Prepare to Be Asked

Remember, of course, that asking is two-way street. When you ask, you must be prepared to be asked, as well. And, if you expect an honest response, you'd best give one, yourself. Remember the feelers. And even if she doesn't ask a single question about your life, it wouldn't hurt for you to share a bit of what you're going through - to share a bit of your happy moments, or sad. But, here again, remember that telling your story is not the point. The point is to demonstrate genuine interest and establish authentic connection. The point is to let this emerging young woman know that you are authentically interested in who she is and what she's going through.

Then, when things do get crazy – and you know they will - you have a precedent for asking, "What's going on?" You'll have an at-least-partially-opened door through which you can both move into a discussion of the craziness. Now, unless you are the girl's therapist, it's not wise to try to be one. Best that you are what you are, be it teacher, parent or friend. Best that you are precisely who you are, as one who cares about what's going on in this girl's life. And, as we have mentioned several times before, this honest connection will benefit you, the adult, at least as much, if not more than it benefits the girl.

Ask in Small Groups
Middle-school girls love to talk with each other in small groups about almost anything, not the least of which is about what's going on in their lives. Listen in on a group of middle-school girls over pizza or on a camping trip or after a big day at the beach or in the back of car and you can hear whirlwind conversations about almost anything.

At Hanger Hall, we have advisor/advisee times every week. (See Chapter 1) Believing in the efficacy of small groups and the unqualified value of providing a place for our students to talk and share about what they are going through, the girls get to pick a teacher whom they want as their advisor. They get to choose three; and we try to make sure that their advisor is one of those three.

Then, each week, the advisors get together with their advisees just to talk about "stuff." Sometimes they go out on a picnic. Sometimes they have some sort of project to do together: make a birthday card for someone, cook a new dish for every one to try, plan a party, pick up trash… whatever. Sometimes, they go to someone's home or, often, just find a private, cozy place at School.

The point of advisor/advisee time is to simply be together with a not-necessarily-academic agenda, and to allow the students the chance to talk about whatever they want to talk about. It is a chance for the teacher to ask how things are going at school and at home or with friends. It is in advisor/advisee times that we often get hints of a particular struggle that's going on. We get a sense of hard feelings that may be emerging or worries or anxieties that are getting played out. In advisor/advisee time, teachers can learn just how much a girl is enjoying her life and what's going well. They can learn what's bringing excitement and enthusiasm into her picture. It's a place to learn what new friends she has discovered and what she is learning about herself.

But, more than that, advisor/advisee time provides a safe place for girls to share their feelings and ideas in a small, caring group. These regular external connections give ample opportunity to share and process some of the remarkable and confusing internal connections that are going on every moment at the speed of light.

Name the Feeling

Something we have found to be extremely helpful has been to invite students to name their feelings. Middle-school girls are fast developing the capability to think abstractly and reflect on multiple perspectives (See Chapter 3). With this emerging ability, these girls can now begin to identify their feelings. They can begin to give names to their emotions and mindsets. "Are you feeling sad?" a teacher might ask. "What kind of sad? How is this sad different from other sadness?" And, when they discover their ability to define and identify their inner sensations, they discover a new power within themselves to deal with their feelings.

When you name something, you automatically have a sense of management or control over that which is named. It's as if you know it or know something about it. Naming something puts you in relationship with it and allows you to deal with it. We have found that when a girl names her feelings, she often discovers a strength she didn't know she had; and she may begin to realize that she doesn't have to live her life at the mercy of her feelings.

Travel: A Great Time for Reflection

There's nothing like getting away from what is familiar to reflect about what is familiar. At Hanger Hall, we are big on travel. (See Chapter 9) We take a wide variety of field trips through out the School year; and take one big trip with each grade during the year. We have gone to Charleston, South Carolina to explore history, barrier islands and cultural mindsets. We have gone to the Florida Keys to snorkel, dive and study marine biology. We have gone to New York to take in museums, Broadway shows, American history. We have gone to Mexico and spent time in a Mexican middle school, as well as exploring ruins, hot springs and Mexican history.

And what we have discovered in travel with the girls is, that, not only do the girls learn a wide variety of new skills, new ideas and information; but, they also learn new ideas about themselves, about their home, about their own culture. When you take a middle-school girl out of her comfort zone, but keep her safe, startling new self-discoveries happen daily. A few years earlier - when the girl was 7, 8 or 9 years old – the experience would be nowhere near the same. But, during these amazing years of pubescence, when cognitive, social, mental and physical growth is happening by the moment, travel can be one of the greatest tools imaginable for a girl to reflect on her self - to realize who she is and who she is becoming.

When we have these girls away from home, we spend lots of time in small groups with a teacher or two, asking questions: What have you learned today? What have you learned about yourself today? We encourage the girls to write in their travel journal, perhaps compose a poem or draw a picture. We sometimes find a beautiful spot where we ask the girls to simply find a comfortable place, sit quietly and "think about the top three things that are most important to you right now," or "think about how you're different now than you were a year ago," or "think how you would like to make this world a better place."

Asking questions is one of the best ways to not only show a middle school girl that you are interested in her life, but, to demonstrate to her that her life is interesting - worth exploring and examining. Asking questions can help an emerging young woman ask herself questions. Asking questions can go a long way in developing new critical thinking skills and in offering her the tools to assess her self and her surroundings for the rest of her life.

B) Listen

The necessary corollary to asking, of course, is listening. And just as the asking needs to come from a genuine concern, so does the listening.

This asking/listening guideline seems so obvious, on the one hand. On the other, when feelings get edgy and anxiety is on the rise, parents and teachers can easily forget to ask and listen and resort instead to directives, orders and commands. If your middle-schooler is on the defensive for whatever reason and you come back at her with your own defenses, you have the makings for a train wreck, or, at the very least, a lose-lose power play.

Asking and listening can diffuse defensiveness, anxiety and even anger more quickly than just about anything else. If your 12-year-old daughter storms into the house after school, slamming doors and barking a greeting; and you respond with your own barked command not to slam the doors and to be more polite, you can almost guarantee that the battle lines will have been drawn and whatever she is feeling and whatever you are feeling, have both escalated.

If, on the other hand, you allow her to slam her way into her room, give her a little space and then calmly and genuinely ask, "What's going on?" – as opposed to and angry, "WHAT'S GOING ON!!!" - the situation might just de-escalate and you both might begin the process of moving-through rather than walling-up.

But, once the question is asked, there had better be some listening time programmed in - some authentic listening time. If you ask the question, "What's going on?" there had better be some listening time that is rooted exclusively in a genuine concern for "what's going on." As in, what's going on deep inside? As in, what's going on her daily life? As in, what's going on in the life of this precious and irreplaceable young girl/woman, whom you are privileged to parent and teach?

Listen For What She Says, Not For What You Want To Hear
If listening is to truly work, it's got to be truely listening. No matter how outlandish, peculiar, convoluted, unreasonable or infuriating her answers or responses might be, the point is to listen - to really hear what she says. And, if you don't understand exactly what she's saying, ask again. Ask in another way. Let her know that you are willing to hear anything she has to tell you. Even, and sometimes, especially, unpleasant information.

As you listen, pace yourself. Remember that this girl before you is going through profound changes in her life on a daily basis. Change is the operative word. She is modifying, adjusting, transforming, amending. She is adding, subtracting, multiplying and dividing her way of thinking, her way of understanding, her way of feeling, her sense of who she is. So, when she tells you things you don't want to hear, remember that much of the bad news will take care of itself. Obviously, if she tells you that she thinks she's pregnant or has been using drugs or alcohol, you may have to take some action. But, take it later. When she is talking to you, more often than not, she wants an ally and a friend. She wants a trusted partner with whom she can move through her difficult times.

When you hear, "I hate my friend," or "School sucks, " or "I'm fat and ugly," or "You never let me do anything," remember that by tomorrow morning, some of these feelings will have lifted. Some of these feelings will even have totally turned around. Change is what's happening within. Change is what's happening without. The operative word here is "change." Yes, things can change for the worse; and they may just do that for a while. But, finally, change is your ally. The fact that change is real means that there is hope.

At Hanger Hall, we start the year with three days at a summer camp. (See Chapter 1) All of us - faculty, administration, students. We stay in cabins together. We eat together, do ropes courses together, do talent shows, horseback riding, canoeing, swimming - all as a way of building community. During this camp a few years ago, one of the teachers overheard a new 6th grader say, "I already hate this school. None of my friends are here and I don't like doing any of these camp things."

The teacher shared that information with a couple of the other teachers. So, a few hours later, after supper, one of the teachers pulled the girl aside and asked, "How do you like Hanger Hall so far?"

"Love it!" the girl responded.

"Oh," said the teacher, "that's wonderful. Somebody had told me that you didn't like it; so I thought I'd better check."

"Oh, that was this afternoon," the girl said. "I was just mad."

When you're dealing with middle-school girls, it's always good to have the awareness of lots of "change" awareness in your pocket.

Reflective Listening? Yes, if It's Authentic.

Years ago, reflective listening was all the rage among marriage counselors. The idea of reflective listening was to reflect back precisely what you hear, as a way of 1) making sure you are hearing correctly; and 2) making sure the person to whom you are listening knows that you are hearing what is being said.

Sometimes, reflective listening works wonders. Sometimes, it becomes so awkward and artificial that the conversation can break down. When you respond to everything your middle-school girl says with, "What I hear you saying, is…" the conversation can become so stilted and uncomfortable that no one wants to be there anymore.

If you're her teacher, you must be her teacher. If you're her parent, you must be her parent. Life is confusing enough for your middle-school girl not to have to figure out who you are and what you are trying to be. In the midst of whatever emotional upheaval she's going through, she doesn't need to wonder if you are suddenly trying to become her psychologist, minister or mediator.

It is over-archingly imperative that, as parent, teacher, coach, group leader or whatever, that you be yourself – albeit, your most compassionate and caring self. Be the self who - more than anything – wants this amazing and irreplaceable middle-school girl to grow into a healthy, strong and capable young woman. And, once again, remember that middle-school girls have feelers that can stretch to the moon and back again. You will not fool her for long, if you fool her at all.

Asking and Listening in School.
One of the best lessons we teach at Hanger Hall is the power each of us has to deal with our challenges. If an issue comes up within a class regarding personalities, conflicts, hurt feelings, perceived injustice - whatever it may be - the teacher has the option to put the academic lesson on hold and move into a problem-solving session right then and there. A problem-solving session is simply a time in which the students are given the chance to name the problem, examine the problem and offer solutions to the problem within a given time limit.

If there is a hurt feeling, for example, or if one of the girls has said something upsetting to another, the students are offered the opportunity to say exactly what happened - to question the one who felt hurt, and the one who said the offensive words. Teachers report that when this happens in an open and honest way, issues are almost always solved or at least moved towards solution. The girls – if given the chance – come up with a resolution to whatever the problem was. And the key to the success of this open discussion is asking and listening, remembering that each person may have a different observation of what happened or what might happen and working together demonstrates that they have the power to take charge of problems and the ability to work through them.

We have done this even with the entire student body and, depending upon the issue, we inevitably have rapt and silent attention. The girls know when they are truly being trusted with their thoughts and expressions. And the end result is, not only a solution, but a lesson of strength and capability.

Listen to Your Self
OK, this can be a challenge. While you are in conversation with your middle-school girl and listening as well as you can, it can be ever so helpful if you listen to yourself along the way. Listen to the words and phrases you use. Listen to how much you say as opposed to how much she is saying. Listen to your tone of voice. Once again: Listen to your tone of voice.

Marshall McLuhan was a Canadian educator during the last part of the 20th century. His amazingly influential book, *Understanding Media*, (1964, Routledge Press) should be on the required reading list for every teacher and parent who is interested in how media affects the lives of their children.

One of the key concepts of McLuhan's work is, "the medium is the message." The idea is that how something is expressed is more affective than what is expressed. How you say your words, how you appear, how you hold your body, how you smell, how you come across, affects the listener more than what you say. Content can be understood, assimilated and remembered; but how you express that content is what impacts and affects the listener. It's what makes the most lasting impression.

Think of your favorite teacher in elementary school. Chances are, you cannot remember anything in particular that he or she taught you. You probably can't remember the tests that were given, the papers you wrote, the projects you were involved with. More than likely, the reason this favorite teacher was your favorite, was because of the way this teacher taught - his or her tone of voice, manner of speaking, body language. This teacher was probably your favorite not because you learned math, science or spelling, but because of the way you were taught math, science or spelling. This teacher was probably your favorite because he or she was funny or kind or exciting or compassionate or maybe just good-looking.

The same is true in regard to your interaction with your middle-school girl, or with anyone, for that matter. Hence, the need to listen to yourself as you speak - to pay attention to your body language, your facial expressions, whether you are eye-to-eye, standing above or sitting below - to be attentive to how quick your responses may be or how long your responses are. The point here is that simply showing an interest makes an impact. Simply demonstrating that you care conveys a message. And, genuinely listening to your middle-school girl - even as you listen to yourself – can be one of the most significantly life-changing things you can do.

Remember: You Have Feelings Too

In trying to be the best parent or teacher your middle-schooler could ever have… in trying to deal with the wild and wooly feelings that your middle-schooler is experiencing every day, sometimes, it's all too easy to forget that you have feelings, too. You have all kinds of feelings. In dealing with these young, emerging adults on a day-to-day basis, your emotional bank has to endure significant deposits and withdrawals.

Then, of course, there are the emotions involved in your own life - emotions revolving around your spouse or partner or your lack of spouse or partner. You have emotions emerging from your job, your health, your finances, your friends. You have emotions emerging from watching your parents age, from watching yourself age, from watching the news. So many emotions, so little time.

So, in dealing with your middle-schooler's feelings, it's vital to not forget your own. It's imperative not to forget that when her emotions are flying all over the place because of something that happened at school, yours may be in a dither as well because of an unpleasant doctor's diagnosis you just heard about a loved one or a letter you just got from the IRS. Or whatever.

If you want to deal with your middle-schooler's feelings in helpful and healthy way, it is essential that you find a healthy way or ways to deal with yours. It might be with a therapist, minister, friend or mate. It might be through journaling, yoga, walks in the woods or vacations. It might be through art or music, pottery or bird-watching; but, by intentionally dealing with your own feelings, it not only enables you to better deal with your middle-schooler's feelings, it also provides an excellent example to your middle-schooler that you care about yourself and that responsible adults take care of themselves. Your feelings - and how you deal with them – can make a world of difference in how you deal with your middle-school girls.

Bear in mind, as well, that you are always and forever a role model. Not just in areas of morality and ethics, you are a role model in every aspect of life. You are the medium for a most-important message. So, without saying a word, the very way you deal with your feelings is sending a message to your middle-schooler. And that message is: This is one way that adults deal with their feelings. This is one way that, as an adult, you can deal with your feelings.

I know. I know. That's a lot of pressure. But, it's part of the picture. And it's vital that you, as parent or teacher, remember that you are modeling for this young emerging adult in every – make that EVERY – aspect of living.

Dealing With Feelings

- *Seven* -
SOCIAL SKILLS

Hanger Hall is a place where everyone talks to everyone, and no one is left out. - 8th grader

You're shopping in a grocery store; and, as you wheel through the produce section, you see a woman you haven't seen in years. She has a maybe-two-year-old in her shopping cart seat and a maybe-four-year-old walking beside her. The two-year-old is performing the classic "I haven't had my nap and I don't want to be here," whine, while the four-year-old is simply walking quietly beside Mom.

"Helen!" you say, as you approach her (fortunately remembering her name), "I haven't seen you in years. And who are these little lovelies?"

"Oh, my goodness!" Helen responds. "It's been so long. Since I saw you last, I have gotten married and now as you see, have a family."

At that point, the baby – noticing that you, a stranger, is approaching stops herself in mid-whine, turns to you, mouth agape and gawks at you with the perfect catatonic stare. If you had been an alien dressed as bunny rabbit suddenly beaming in from a parallel universe, the stare would be no different.

At the same time that baby sister goes into her stupor, big brother grabs Mama's leg as if it were a tree and does everything he can to hide himself behind it.

"They are so precious," you say. "It must make you proud." You chat a bit about the past, talk tentatively about getting together for lunch (both of you knowing, of course, that with two young children, her chances of going out for lunch are right up there with time-travel and getting drunk with the Pope.) You finish your conversation and wheel your buggy away, realizing that, never once did the 2-year-old even blink in her stupefied stare at you, nor did big, bad bro ever show even a modicum of interest in actually facing you or saying, "Hello."

But neither of these diminutive social blunder-busses bother you in the least. And why? because of their ages. You are fully aware that age – and age alone – grants forgiveness in this regard. Only someone who didn't know children would hang the "rude" or "impolite" label on these kids for socially inept behavior.

Not so with a middle-school girl or boy. By the age of 10-11, most children are expected not to gape silently at strangers or hide behind their mothers' legs. Even without knowing the results of a multi-million dollar research project on the subject, it would be safe to say, that, by the age of 10-11, children in most cultures around the world are generally expected to have learned and appropriated at least a few of the social skills practiced by adults in their communities. Children of middle school age (unless they are mentally or emotionally challenged) should have acquired at least some of the basic and appropriate social skills of their own adult communities. But, sometimes, they haven't.

Socialization Happens

Talk to any college kid who has studied Sociology 101 and he or she will tell you that socialization is what happens when someone grows up in society. Socialization is the process by which people learn how the society around them operates. Socialization does not have to be programmed or taught in school. Socialization is not tested on the EOG's. There are no socialization clubs, classes, cults or churches. No weekend workshops promise to socialize you. Socialization simply happens. It happens constantly. It happens inevitably.

Socialization happens at school. It happens at church, mosque or synagogue. It happens at the family dinner table and the day care center. It happens at birthday parties, slumber parties, pizza parties, cocktail parties. It happens at weddings and funerals, baptisms and bar mitzvahs and family reunions. It happens on the stage at the school play and during a time-out punishment.

Socialization is what happens - what always happens - when people get together. Whenever you see a child in any kind of gathering - anywhere, anytime, for any reason – you can be certain that socialization is going on. It was going on in that grocery-store encounter you had with your old friend. Though that 2 and 4-year-old had no idea of – or interest in – what was going on, you can be sure that their young minds were taking in this exchange, and, in some astounding way, logging the experience into the "what adults do" part of their sponge-like brains.

No matter who you are or where you grew up, if you grew up in society – any society – you were socialized. You were taught by observation. You were taught by example. You were taught by stern, disapproving looks and by proud pats on the back. You were taught by what people laughed at and what made people frown. You were taught by hugs and touches, silences and rowdiness, smells and tastes, music and art.

You Are a Role Model. Always.
With socialization, everyone and everything is a teacher: parents, neighbors, strangers, mailmen, baby-sitters, playmates, store clerks, restaurant waiters. The real people with whom your child has encounters – any kind of encounter – are, each and all, socializing that child. And, though there is some dispute in this matter among educators and psychologists, you can be pretty certain that whatever your child watches on television and movies… whatever your child reads in books… whatever your child sees in plays, concerts or performances… each and all is, in some way, socializing that young being. Everything a child encounters is teaching and training that emerging adult how the world operates - what you're supposed to do and what you're not. Every interactive or observed event teaches what's the right way to think and what's the wrong. It teaches what gets you punished and what gets you applause. It teaches what is considered worthwhile and what is a waste a time.

It can be a humbling and frightening thought for teachers and parents, that whatever you do – what ever you do – is socializing the young lives who are in your presence. You are a role model and your young charges are watching you closely. Every word, every action, every silence, every inaction is socializing the child(ren) in your presence. In simply being who you are, you are instructing these young sponges how the world works and how people work in the world. When you are concerned that your children are "hanging out with the wrong crowd," you may well have a valid concern. Whomever a child spends time with is, inevitably, socializing that child and teaching that child how the world operates. As teacher or parent, coach, group or church leader, that child is spending a big chunk of time with you. You are always modeling.

Social Skills Don't Just Happen

If socialization is what happens to you as you grow up in society, social skills are what you learn along the way. Rather, sometimes you learn. When it comes to living in society, social skills are the tools of the trade. Socialization teaches you how society operates; social skills are the means by which you operate in society. Social skills are as crucial to someone living in society as a hammer, saw, drill and plumb line are to a carpenter. You may know what a house looks like or even how to build a house; but you'll never get it done without the tools.

Just as hormones act as cell phones, enabling one cell in the body to communicate with another, social skills enable you to make connections with other parts of your world. Whether it be interaction in business, education, friendships, relationships, religious groups or with a stranger on the street, social skills open the doors and grease the wheels of communication. Social skills set out the welcome mat and take it in. Social skills lock and unlock the gate. Social skills establish a link and a basis for affiliation and non-affiliation. Social skills provide the feng shui for all kinds of contacts, connections, links, liaisons and boundaries.

Quite often, social skills are learned from example. A child will tend to model her behavior after the significant adults and peers in her life. Teachers and parents need to realize that as important as they are in modeling behavior, they are, far and away, not the only ones teaching their children social skills. Likewise, simply because parents and teachers are modeling doesn't mean the children are following.

Many times, children view adult behavior as adult behavior - meant to be practiced solely by adults. Children understand quite clearly that different rules apply to them. Adults aren't normally told when to get ready for bed or to clean up their plates or to make their beds or straighten their rooms. As far as children know, adults never have anyone telling them how to dress or when they can go out and play or how much television they can watch. As far as children can see, adults are never reprimanded or put in time-out unless it's by the law. And, most certainly, adults are never spanked. So, it's easy for a child to assume that because the rules are different for adults, then adult behavior is different, as well. So, just because mom says, "hello" to the neighbor every morning when she goes out to get the paper, doesn't mean that children should have to say, "hello" or anything, for that matter. Quite often, from a child's point of view, there are two distinct worlds - adults and kids. And, it is often assumed by a child that different rules and different sets of behavior apply to each of those worlds.

Hence, the need for social skills to be not just modeled, but consciously and intentionally taught. Modeling is vital. Instruction without example is worthless. "Do what I say; don't do what I do," will never work. But, more often than not, when it comes to social skills, a child must be taught the why and the how-to by a consistent and caring adult, if the skills are to stick.

Keep in mind that your middle-school girl is an emerging adult. She will be a full-blown adult before you know it. She needs all the help she can get to understand and appropriate what it means to be an adult. And the more you can offer her in this regard, the better equipped she will be to navigate the often-tumultuous waters of living as a happy, healthy and successful woman in this world. Social skills are some of the best tools of the trade you can offer her.

Connections and Boundaries

Social skills not only enable connections to happen, they can help make boundaries clear. And these two elements – establishing connections and setting boundaries - are two of the most vital, useful and necessary skills a young, emerging woman can learn.

Developmentally, one of the most important things that is happening with a middle-school girl is an emerging healthy sense of self – a process of self-definition. Social skills help define who you are – offer the boundaries to help define who you are. Social skills can help make it quite clear where you stand and where you don't. Social skills make it possible to express yourself comfortably and in a forthright manner. Social skills say, "This is the way I do things. This is the way I operate. This is how I am comfortable in connecting. This is where I draw the line." A young woman who is comfortable in expressing who she is, is a young woman who will move through her days with far more grace and ease than one who lacks that ability. Social skills are some of the tools which raise that comfort level.

By the time a girl reaches the age of 10-11, she has a fair sense of who she is and who she isn't. She is usually quite clear by this age, for example, that she is:
1) a girl and not a boy;
2) a certain height and weight;
3) a particular skin and hair color;
4) a part of a family and network of friends;
5) in a certain grade in school;
6) fond of certain foods, certain music, certain movies, books, activities, people, animals, subjects in school, clothes… and not fond of others;
7) no longer a little girl, but not yet a woman.

In many ways, a middle school girl has a sharp sense of her boundaries and her connections. But, in coming to terms of a bigger picture - of a world of limitless possibilities, discovery and danger – a middle school girl usually has a long way to go.

By the age of 10-11, for example, a girl may or may not be aware:

1) that her way of thinking about the world is expanding every day: that how she sees the world today may be radically different from how she sees it tomorrow;

2) that everyone is not watching and judging her all the time;

3) that her gifts, talents, personality and mind will finally serve her better than her physical beauty;

4) that there are many people in the world who will help and teach her;

5) that there are a few who may try to take advantage of her;

6) that she is particularly adroit in certain areas of life and challenged in others;

7) that over the next 2-3 years, her entire physical appearance and mental abilities will be changing dramatically;

8) of her innate abilities to adapt and grow with change;

9) of how her spiritual leanings may reflect or differ from her parents'.

In other words, she still needs experience and guidance to enable her to find deeper, wider connections and clearer, well-defined and healthy boundaries. She has much to learn and much of which to be aware. The middle-school years are a time of fleshing out some of these "awarenesses."

These years offer an incredible (and some say, once-in-a-lifetime) opportunity to for a girl to a) develop and expand her consciousness of the world around and within her; b) to assimilate or discard certain ideas of how life works; c) to come to terms with what is going on within herself and her environment, and d) to find ways and learn to use the tools to move through this profoundly dynamic and expanding time of her life. Social skills are some of the best tools available for navigating these amazing and tumultuous waters of the middle-school years.

The Top Ten Social Skills (A Starter List)

The opening words of the Hanger Hall School Pledge, are: As a Hanger Hall girl, I will be kind, honest and respectful to myself and all others. Kind, honest and respectful. These words sum up the primary reasons underlying many of the social skills we feel are vital for middle-school girls to learn and practice. But, we have found, that in their practice, these skills provide a plethora of benefits for the girls and for all who come in contact with them.

There are, of course, volumes of social skills that can be taught and practiced. Hanger Hall is no finishing school. The following ten skills, however, are what we teach, practice and model on a regular basis. The descriptions that follow are similar to those we use with our students. They are clear, concise and easily understood by middle school girls. We highly recommend them to all teachers and parents of middle school girls.

One very effective way of teaching these skills is by letting the parents of our students know exactly what social skills we are teaching their daughters: the why and the how. Then we encourage the parents to follow-through and reinforce these skills by regularly and consciously practicing them with their daughters at home.

1& 2) Greetings and Farewells

A forthright, "Hello" or, parting, "Goodbye," establishes quite clearly the boundaries of your involvement in a conversation or group meeting. A solid greeting makes it ever so clear that you are opening the lines of communication – that you are willing to make a connection with the person(s) present. A clear greeting lets everyone know of your presence – that you are not hiding in the shadows, but ready for what is to follow. A good, "Hello," expresses a sense of self-assurance and comfort in being who you are and where you are.

By the same token, an unambiguous and friendly, "Goodbye," honors the person(s) present in the conversation that you care about them enough to say a farewell. Keep in mind that "Goodbye," is, simply an abbreviated form of the phrase, "God be with ye." So, in saying, "Goodbye," you are offering a kind of blessing. Likewise, a formal farewell, as opposed to simply slipping away unnoticed, is a statement of self-assurance: You were OK being there; you are OK in leaving.

Note: We teach that when entering or leaving a larger group situation, greetings and farewells should be addressed to the host, hostess or person in charge of the meeting, rather than trying to address everyone present.

3) Eye Contact

If eyes are the windows of the soul, one of the best ways to get to know someone would be to look in their eyes. Likewise, when you offer your eyes to another and look directly at them, you are saying without words, "I am willing to honestly share this time with you: willing to listen carefully to you and offer what I can." Making eye contact says, "I am not ashamed of myself. I am OK with who I am." Making eye contact is a non-verbal way of expressing inner strength and genuine openness.

We encourage our students to practice this eye contact, not just with each other, but with adults. And it works! Again and again, we have people tell us that having a conversation with one of our girls is unlike almost any conversation with the average 12 year-old. "These girls actually look at you and talk to you!" we are told by parents and visitors to the school.

4) Showing Interest

Everyone wants to feel important. Everyone wants to feel special in some way. One of the best ways to acknowledge that another person is important, is to show interest in their activities, their feelings, their hopes and dreams. "What have you been doing today?" can be a far better conversation starter than, "How's it going?" Particularly, if you follow the first question with another: "What kind of work have you been doing?" And so forth. "Have you done anything fun lately?" can also get the conversation rolling.

What makes this social skill really work is following one question with another. Some folks like to ask an opening cliché question and then immediately start talking about themselves. Someone skilled in social behavior will usually endeavor to get the others talking first and then share his or her own story. Likewise, in a group conversation, some folks are more reticent to speak than others. A good question directed here and there can open things up and get the chatter flowing.

If you truly show an interest in another person or persons, it is almost guaranteed that you will end up having a fine conversation. Some one has said, "If you talk with someone – no matter who it is – and don't end up learning something, then you haven't been paying attention." Asking questions and showing interest helps you learn.

5) Introductions

Yes, you are important. Yes, you have much to offer. But, in a conversation, classroom or group meeting, you're not the only player. If it's truly a conversation you are having with another person(s), then, each one has lines to speak. Each one has something to share. And, no matter how fascinating, compelling and hilarious your life may be, one of the best social skills you can learn in conversation, is to share the stage - to hear what other people have to say, to truly listen and respond from an interested point of view.

Nor is your role simply to be quiet and listen or to ask question after question to get the others talking. Sharing the stage simply means sharing. You have lines to speak. You have stories to tell; and so do the others who are with you in conversation.

6) Sharing the Stage

Everyone wants to feel important - important enough to be greeted, important enough to be heard, important enough to be introduced. If you are talking with one person and another walks into the conversation, introductions are always appropriate. If you know the names of both, then the ball would fall into your court to introduce the two of them. But even if you don't know names, it's always good to offer the chance for introductions. And, even if you feel as if they have already met each other, it is far better to offer an introduction than not.

A good, "Hi, my name is _____, and I'd like you to meet _____," with a hand outstretched is one of the most welcoming signs available in our society. It's a sign that says, "You are important. I would like to know you. I bet you have something to offer this conversation." It's a sign that also says, "I am comfortable with who I am. I am comfortable meeting you."

7) Inclusiveness

We had a group of Buddhist monks visit to share some religious and cultural ideas. As part of their visit, we had prepared a small buffet-style meal for everyone to enjoy. We offered plates to the monks and invited them to lead the buffet line. Instead, these saffron-robed holy men picked up a stack of plates and passed them around to each of the rest of us in the room. The English-speaking leader said, "We all eat together. That way, we remember we are all together."

Middle-school girls often get the feeling that they are on the outside looking in. Not quite a child anymore, not quite an adult. They can easily believe that they are on the outside of both worlds, looking in. For this, and many other reasons, middle-school girls appreciate being included and understand the need for inclusiveness. They know that no one likes to feel left out. They know that, when they are included in whatever conversation or activity that is happening, they feel accepted. And, being included is often the most important thing that can happen.

A simple, "Come join us!" Or, offering someone a drink, snack or seat at a gathering can make all the difference in the interaction that is to follow. If a person can be welcomed and made to feel "at home," that person will almost always have a positive experience in whatever arena it may be.

8) Kind Words

There's a line in the classic Disney movie, "Bambi," in which Thumper's (a young rabbit's) mother says, "Thumper, if you can't say something nice about someone, don't say anything at all." Good advice. At Hanger Hall, rather than simply discouraging gossip or making fun of someone behind backs, we advocate using kind words when we are speaking about another person. Rather than simply not speaking well of another, we encourage the students to find ways of speaking kindly. The use of kind words is, of course, a most excellent exercise for people of all ages. We suggest that students not say anything about another person which they would not say in the presence of that person.

Middle school girls often go through their days assuming that they are constantly being watched or judged by someone, about practically everything. The way they dress, the way their parents dress, the way their hair is fixed, the kind of book bag they carry, the tone of their voices – everything is out there being judged, appraised, evaluated, considered. So, when a girl finds herself in a group of students and cruel critiques are being made about another girl who is not present, it's easy for her to assume that such judgments will be made somewhere, sometime about her, as well. And the result can be that each of the girls walk away from such an experience with far more self-consciousness and far less self-assurance. We remind our girls at Hanger Hall that even a few kind words can change everything about the way someone feels about herself.

We recommend to our students that they join The Compliment Club. It's a Club that brings its members a high degree of satisfaction and happiness. The Club has no dues, no meetings, not even a membership list. The way you join is quite simple: You become an active member of The Compliment Club when you offer three honest compliments to some person or persons some time during the day. The compliments can be about anything: clothes, smiles, tone of voice, friendliness, abilities in sports or academics - anything at all. We remind our students that, if they're having a bad day, one of the best things you can do to feel better is to join The Compliment Club.

9) Body Language

We teach our girls that, before they utter a word to another person, they have already communicated with their bodies. Middle-school girls are often overly conscious of their bodies, but, usually, it's about how their bodies look, not what they are expressing. Seldom does the average middle-school girl regard her body as a primary way of communicating. We teach our students that how they sit, stand, walk and carry themselves communicates a great deal about who they are and how they feel about themselves.

We remind our students that:
- Poor posture or slumped shoulders can communicate, "I don't think very highly about myself. I don't think I have much to offer this conversation," or "I really don't want to be here."
- Crossed arms can communicate, "I'm feeling angry, resentful and defensive. You'd better have something worthwhile to say."
- Looking around during a conversation rather than making eye contact, can say, "I'm really not interested in what you are talking about and the sooner you finish saying it, the better."
- Fidgeting with hands, hair, pencil or whatever expresses nervousness, discomfort, anxiety or uneasiness.

At Hanger Hall, we feel it is important not only for girls to be aware of how they communicate to others with their bodies; but we encourage the girls to read their own body language as a way of discovering what it is they are feeling.

10) Speaking Your Voice

The phrase "learning to speak your voice" is a popular catch phrase for many authors, educators and psychologists. "Learning to speak your voice" can mean to speak from your heart, to speak from what is true for you. To speak your voice may mean to speak with a sense of who you are, not just what the other person wants to hear or wants you to be.

If you are learning to speak your voice, "learning" is the operative word. Very few adults would claim that every word they speak comes from their heart. We are all (hopefully) learning to speak more genuinely and express ourselves more authentically. But middle school is prime time for beginning this learning process. The middle school years are inexpressibly important in the development of a sense of who you are and how you are unique in this world. These are the years when you determine how you are different-from and same-as other people. Learning to speak your voice - or even beginning to learn - is one of the best exercises we can offer our girls to enhance this crucial development.

Now, of course, when teachers ask for an answer in, say, math or history class, they would much rather hear an answer which comes from the student's head rather than her heart. You would much rather hear something that comes from her cognitive study and research rather than her emotive feelings. But, learning to speak even in the academic arena is a way of learning to speak your voice.

We teach our students that simply speaking clearly and confidently - about whatever subject - can help you learn to speak your voice. We encourage our students to articulate and not mumble - to speak whatever they have to say with as much clarity as possible.

Keeping the Main Thing the Main Thing

Whether it's teaching math, science, Spanish, art, history, humanities or social skills, it is important to remember what we are doing with our children. Sometimes, we parents and teachers can get so pumped up on whatever it is we want our emerging young women to learn, that we forget what treasures they are; and that, finally, what we are trying to offer these treasures, are tools for the trade of living.

Social skills are important, but they are not the Holy Grail. Nor are "A's" in every subject. When we take any of these academic subjects or developmental concepts more seriously than we take the joy of living or the individual wonder of each of our lives, then we have surely missed the mark.

What we want to impart to our students is that, like a voyage at sea, life can be wild and wonderful, terrifying and challenging; but it's all right, because there are tools for the journey. There are maps and compasses, rudders and sails. There are ways to tie knots and ways to steer into the wind that can grant the passage a grace and ease, which might not happen otherwise. Social skills are some of those maps, compasses, rudders and sails that can get you where you need to be; but they're not what the journey is about.

Social Skills

- Eight -
MOVING FORWARD
(THEORETICALLY SPEAKING)

I have gotten a lot less shy. Ask anyone. – Millie, grade 7

The theories of Piaget (See Chapter 3) and Erikson (Chapter 5) are far-reaching and powerful. As we already noted, however, that does not mean they are perfect. This chapter presents three more recent theoretical approaches. The first one, Fowler's theory of faith development, represents both a combination and an expansion of Piaget and Erikson. The other two represent entirely new ways of describing certain aspects of development. All of them provide valuable insights, and all of them are well- represented in the educational approach adopted by Hanger Hall.

What Makes a Good Theory?

Good theories are like community gardens. In both cases, extensive work is required on the front end. For a comprehensive theory, data must be gathered, the available literature must be analyzed, current knowledge must be synthesized in a new way, and innovative thinking must be published. For a community garden, a site must be found, leaders must be identified, ownership agreements must be drawn up, and membership rules must be determined.

Presumably, the benefits outweigh the effort. Good theories provide a common language for discussing casual observations and research findings. They offer a framework for analyzing and contemplating data. They supply overarching themes (See also Introduction). Community gardens create a common space that brings folks together. They offer opportunities for urbanites to get back in touch with the land. They provide color, nourishment, and joy to a district.

Both, however, function well only if they represent a true communal effort. Many people know that researchers are supposed to publish their findings. Even people outside of the university system have heard the phrase "publish or perish." The reason publishing scholarly work is so important is that the entire intellectual enterprise relies on ideas being placed into the public domain. Criticism, debate, assessment, and evaluation are integral parts of the process, but the work must be available to others for that to happen. Similarly, gardens that aren't shared become backyard plots. There's nothing wrong with individual efforts, but something built by, and for, a community is quite a different entity.

The implication is that theories, like those of Piaget and Erikson, become influential largely because intellectual peers appreciate their significance. These theories account for good portions of the current data. They hold up over time. They apply to different ethnic groups, cultures, and environments. If not, they are adaptable. When Piaget's assigned ages seemed questionable, adjustments were made. When his number of stages seemed inadequate, the theory was tweaked (See Chapter 3).

Good theories also provide jumping off points for future researchers. Freud's theory is almost never fully accepted in its original form by modern psychologists, but his impact can still be felt. His students include a long list of famous psychologists, including Jung, who developed their own far-reaching theories. The fields of art, literature, and philosophy have all been impacted by psychoanalytical theory. And many of the "psychological terms" used in our everyday language, like "oral fixation" or "anal-retentive" stem from Freudian theory. Piaget laid the groundwork for innumerable studies in diverse cultures and in a range of school setting. Likewise, Erikson's concept of identity formation has led to years of additional work on self-esteem, self-consciousness, and emotionality (See Chapter 5). Together, they provided the foundation for a theory of spiritual development.

Spiritual Development
One obvious omission in early developmental theories was an explicit statement

about spirituality. Psychology has expended almost no resources in studying spiritual development. We can't describe how children create or revise god-images over the course of development. We've published almost no research on how children establish an overarching life philosophy. Even relatively simply questions, like how children view their religious upbringing as it is happening to them, remain largely unanswered.

Ironically, parents from around the world recognize that spiritual development is an important part of the maturational process. In one recent study,[1] researchers associated with the Center for Spiritual Development, conducted interviews with parents from several countries, including Australia, China, India, Israel, and Nigeria. Diverse traditions, including Buddhism, Christianity, Hinduism, Judaism, and Sikhism were also represented. Despite the differences, parents generally agreed that spirituality plays an important role in raising successful adults. They also agreed that families can foster spiritual growth in a variety of ways. Modeling positive behavior, using rituals, establishing clear boundaries, and practicing a religion were methods frequently mentioned by parents, regardless of ethnicity or religious tradition.

On the plus side, several books about spiritual development have been published in the last few years.[2] The Center for Spiritual Development has outlined a comprehensive plan to study spirituality in children and adolescents around the world. And researchers across disciplines are beginning to recognize the importance of this topic, especially given the "shrinking of the global community." However, it will take years for the data to be collected and analyzed, and comprehensive theories are still lacking.

Fowler's Stages of Faith

James Fowler's book, *Stages of Faith: The Psychology of Human Development and the Quest for Meaning*,[3] represents one early theoretical attempt. It's particularly relevant to this manual because the theory was based on the work of Piaget and

Erikson.[4] It was also based on interviews conducted with over 400 people from a variety of religious and non-religious backgrounds. The youngest interviewee was four years old; the oldest was 88.

Fowler's notion of "faith" represents the human quest for an all-encompassing worldview. This worldview provides us with an approach, an orientation, or a "total response" that we use when interpreting life's events or when reacting to the world around us. Faith gives meaning to our relationships. It provides a purpose for our efforts. It integrates our values and goals. According to this view, faith development is universal; it is experienced by all individuals in the course of their lives. It also transcends religious beliefs and religious practice.

Faith development occurs when we weave our life experiences into a unifying image or narrative. Since those experiences begin at birth (or even before birth), the seeds of faith development are sown at a very young age. Fowler actually refers to this developmental period as a pre-stage when faith is "undifferentiated." During this time, very young infants gain the concept of mutuality. They learn that they are separate from others, but hopefully, they also learn that those others are caring and loving. Fowler clearly did his homework on Erikson since the development of trust (as opposed to mistrust) is an essential building block for Fowler's later faith stages.

Intuitive-Projective Stage

Near the end of life's second year, toddlers begin to assemble a rudimentary faith based on the foundation laid during infancy. This "intuitive-projective" faith is grounded in whatever stories and images are made accessible to the child. Adults may read from sacred texts. Families may attend religious services. Friends may talk about rituals like weddings or funerals. Television characters may refer to a God. Children then use bits and pieces of this culturally-infused knowledge to begin generating a sense of the sacred. Their narratives are still disjointed and disorganized; their images are still fragmented and fantasy-filled. Nevertheless, they are clearly creating early god-images, and they are happy to share their budding wisdom. They refer to God sending signs – like stop signs and peace signs. They imagine that heaven is a place where you go after you die – and before you are born. They describe God as being "like the air" or "all around you." Conceptually, these early views are quite different from those of most adults, but even very young children already appear to be constructing a spiritual sense of meaning about the world around them.

Intuitive-projective faith relies on exactly the type of cognitive development outlined by Piaget – the ability to think in symbols. The term "intuitive-projective" is intended to acknowledge that children are becoming increasingly self-aware and savvy, but they still have a rather simplistic understanding of their environment. With their vivid imaginations, they are only beginning to distinguish fantasy from reality. And their understanding of cultural taboos is minimal. Fowler therefore believed that faith development was both constrained and enhanced by the cognitive abilities of the child. In fact, the age range Fowler assigned to the intuitive-projective stage (2-7 years) matches the age range Piaget assigned to his Preoperational Stage.

Mythic-Literal Stage

Fowler's next faith stage, Mythic-Literal, roughly corresponds to Piaget's Concrete Operations period (ages 7-11). This stage is typical of the early middle-schooler, although Fowler acknowledges that some people continue to exhibit mythic-literal qualities well into adolescence or even adulthood. The stage is marked by children's growing skill in telling stories. Their narratives are more coherent and follow the guidelines of the culture. They have a stronger sense of fairness and justice. They want claims to be supported by tangible evidence. They also tend to use symbols more literally.

Because children in this stage are somewhat more able to recognize the perspectives of others, their stories begin to reflect that their own perspective is unique.

They incorporate individualized experiences and ideas, such as the lessons derived form their own family dynamics. One 10-year-old, when asked if parents always do the right thing, replied, "No, they don't always do the right thing, but they think what they do is best. Sometimes, they make mistakes and I guess God probably makes mistakes too." (p.141) However, children still lack the more adult-like ability to step back and reflect on these perspectives.

Their god-images and god-narratives also tend to exhibit anthropomorphic elements that highlight the human capacities of God. God is now more likely to be described as an old man with white hair and white beard. He sits on a throne in the clouds on top of the world. He pays attention to people and what they're doing. When people are good, God is thoughtful, patient, and compassionate toward them. When people misbehave, God metes out punishments. In short, God, like a parent, does what He thinks is best.

Synthetic-Conventional Stage

During puberty, a new stage of faith often emerges, called synthetic-conventional. Fowler portrays mythic-literal faith as "describing the flow from the midst of the stream" (p.137). He describes synthetic-conventional faith as looking at the flow of the whole stream from the vantage point of the river bank (see p.152). In other words, in the synthetic-conventional stage, adolescents can now step back and reflect on their own faith construction. They can also reflect on the constructions of others. Comparisons can be made, discrepancies can be noted, and value systems can be weighed against one other. Again, this stage of faith clearly relies on the emerging cognitive and social abilities so eloquently described by Piaget and Erikson.

In many cases, adolescents will closely identify with the teachings of their parents. As one teen put it: *My parents have guided me in the right direction.... They brought me to church and taught me about God and love and everything, and now I know what it is and...and I'll be telling my daughter or my son, or whatever, the same thing.* (p.157)

Other teens may begin to differentiate themselves from their parents. In most cases, however, faith constructions still stem from some external, but fairly conventional, authority such as peers, the media, or a church. These adolescents are certainly developing an increasingly personal sense of meaning. However, it is not completely individualized yet because it continues to rely on the expectations and values of others.

In the synthetic-conventional stage, adolescents also begin to rely less on concrete, human-like images of God. Their descriptions tend to focus on feelings or emotions, a transition that makes sense given the onset of abstract reasoning. There is also an increased focus on one's private relationship with God. This God understands the newly-developed self on a deep level. This God recognizes the ideal, possible self of the future. This God serves as a benevolent member of the imaginary audience. Adolescents are now much more likely to describe God as a companion, a guide, a mentor. God takes notice when you are struggling with a problem. God loves you when you feel self-conscious or down and out.

Beyond Synthetic-Conventional

Fowler outlined three additional stages of faith, for a total of six stages, but they almost never apply to middle-schoolers. In fact, many people will remain in the synthetic-conventional stage for the duration of their lives. Others will move into stage 4 (Individuative-Reflective faith). That transition is often precipitated by major life changes during adolescence or early adulthood, such as leaving home to attend college or university. Stage 4 also then serves as another typical stopping point in the faith development process.

So where do schools fit in? Recent polling data suggest that many U.S. parents would not oppose assistance from their local schools. In one CBS News poll,[5] 49% of those surveyed said that they would like to see religious and spiritual values have more influence in the schools than they do now. In another poll,[6] 87% of those surveyed were in favor of public schools setting aside time for a moment of silence. Despite such sentiments, non-religious schools that incorporate faith (not religious) development into their teaching are rare.

Hanger Hall recognizes that most middle-school girls are transitioning from the mythic-literal stage to the synthetic-conventional stage. Travel journals, "Observations," (See Chapter 3) and "Now What?" (Chapter 9) all promote narrative development. Holidays from various traditions are honored and discussed (Chapter 1), allowing the girls to reflect on the similarities and differences of diverse cultural practices. And rituals, like the Circle Dance (Chapter 1), pay tribute to the promise of a new identity.

But beyond the specifics of each stage, Fowler's notion of faith development is really about the search for meaning in one's existence. In this sense, Hanger Hall is in a somewhat unique position. By caring for their teachers/role models (See Chapter 1), by providing a sense of order (Chapter 2), by offering compassion (Chapter 2), and by developing both connections and boundaries (Chapter 7) Hanger Hall provides possible answers to life's most pressing questions. But, the girls are also encouraged to identify their own purpose in life. They learn to establish unique and relevant goals. They participate in community service. In such ways, Hanger Hall facilitates the self-discovery necessary to move forward on one's own faith journey.

Alternative Theoretical Approaches

Sometimes, in an academic discipline, the paradigm shifts. The theoretical pendulum swings. The cultural status quo stretches its neck. Such contextual changes often prompt completely novel viewpoints to emerge. These viewpoints are not built on previous theories. They are not revisions; they are not expansions. Instead, they provide new metaphors and innovative terminology. They meander through slightly different terrain; they lay claim to unexplored territory. In the mid-1900s, two such alternatives to thinking about cognitive development appeared on the scene – the Information Processing Approach and Vygotsky's theory. Both offered a fresh perspective on how to think about thinking. And both have had a huge impact on how psychologists and educators view cognitive development.

I'm a Frenchie, not a Spaniard and proud of it. - Molly, grade 7

Information Processing Approach
Computers and Minds – Do They Really Think Alike?

Interviewer: *HAL, you have an enormous responsibility on this mission, in many ways perhaps the greatest responsibility of any single mission element. You're the brain, and central nervous system of the ship, and your responsibilities include watching over the men in hibernation. Does this ever cause you any lack of confidence?*

HAL: *Let me put it this way, Mr. Amor. The 9000 series is the most reliable computer ever made. No 9000 computer has ever made a mistake or distorted information. We are all, by any practical definition of the words, foolproof and incapable of error.*

The film *2001: A Space Odyssey* was released in 1968. The film contains many layers of meaning and serves as a social commentary on several levels. Certainly one issue the film explores is the link between the computer and the human mind. HAL-9000 is a latest generation super computer that controls the spaceship's mission to Jupiter. In the beginning of the movie, there are five human astronauts on board. Three of them are "in hibernation." HAL is the only entity on the spaceship that knows the true nature of the mission. He is more intelligent, more emotional, and more friendly than any of the humans in the film. He is also the most fully developed character. As the movie progresses, HAL begins to break down. The hibernating humans wake up and outwit the computer. They proceed to dismantle and disconnect HAL, who subsequently dies a slow, agonizing death. One of the astronauts then completes the mission to Jupiter alone.

Stanley Kubrick, director of the movie, was not unique in his curiosity about the similarities and differences between computers and minds. In fact, cognitive psychologists began systematically studying those issues in the 1950s. If our senses – vision, audition, touch, etc. – constantly provide us with information from our environment, then how much data can the brain handle at any one time? How does the brain decide what to pay attention to and what to ignore? How long is information stored in the brain? Based on the answers to such questions, scientists began drawing models to depict how the brain manages all of these tasks. Taken together, these lines of research formed the Information Processing Approach. Even the name itself reflects the influence of technology. For over 50 years now, the fields of computer science and cognitive science have informed each other, and the conclusions have provided powerful clues about how to improve brain function and how to teach material so that it is remembered.

Memory

One of the most fascinating areas of research in the Information Processing field has been on the topic of memory. For example, one of the earliest memory models[7] focused on short term memory and long term memory. Because of the model's influence on the field, these terms are often presented in textbooks and news articles, so many people are familiar with them. Another less-heralded model that has been highly informative for educators focuses on "levels of processing."[8]

The "levels of processing" model suggests that information is more easily remembered if it is stored using a deep level of processing rather than a shallow level of processing. The idea was discovered through a series of studies. Although the details of the studies vary, the basic set-up is the same, and the results have been replicated thousands of times across the country in undergraduate courses as classroom demonstrations.

Here's how it works. The research participants are divided into three groups, but they are not told that they are part of a memory study. All three groups are then shown the same list of words. The first group is asked to process the words in a shallow way – like counting the number of "e's" in each word or indicating whether the word is written in lower-case or upper-case letters. Neither of these tasks is very difficult, and most people are able to complete the job without even paying attention to the words themselves. The second group is asked to do something slightly more complicated – like counting the number of syllables in the words or coming up with a rhyming word. This requires a bit more from the participants, but it's still somewhat shallow. The third group is asked to do something more substantial – like think of a memory associated with the word and record whether the memory is pleasant or unpleasant. This task is intended to represent a deeper level of processing.

After a brief period of distraction (30 seconds to 2 minutes), the participants are told that they will be given a test to see how many words they remember. Once they've recovered from their initial surprise, they get to work. As you might expect, the participants in the third group remember the greatest number of words. The participants in the first group remember the fewest number of words.

The implications for education are clear. Anything that compels, facilitates, or allows for a deeper level of processing will make the information more memorable. Reflecting on academic goals (See Chapter 4), facilitating exploration (Chapter 9), and teaching through travel all promote deep processing. Academic classes (Chapter 10) that are experiential, multisensory, and interdisciplinary ensure solid understanding of the material. Reflective discussions and journaling seal the deal. In short, deep processing is part of the daily routine at Hanger Hall.

Vygotsky: In the Zone
Athletes sometimes talk about being "in the zone." It's the state an athlete wants to be in. There is the feeling that efforts will produce results, that goals are clear and attainable, and that there is some control over the situation. Basketball players drop three-pointers. Baseball batters see the spin on the ball. Quarterbacks talk about the field "slowing down." A similar phenomenon can occur in the mental world as well. The idea that there is a "cognitive space" where learning is at a peak was

proposed by Lev Vygotsky during the early 1900s.[9]

Vygotsky was a Russian psychologist who was also trained as a teacher. His ideas are slightly different from those of athletes or other performers, but the notion that mental performance can be optimized is similar. Like Piaget, Vygotsky was interested in how children learn about the world around them. As an educator, Vygotsky was also highly interested in social interactions. These social interactions could be between children and teachers or between the children themselves.

According to the theory, learning occurs best in the "zone of proximal development." The zone encompasses different aspects of a task to be learned. Take the example of grocery shopping, a fairly complex process, believe it or not. A typical shopping trip would require that a list be written and then used at the store. The shopper needs transportation to the store. Products must be placed into the cart – a process that includes selecting the correct brand and the correct size. Finally, the food is paid for. Cash? Check? Debit? Credit? As we all know, each payment method requires different knowledge. Clearly, a three-year-old can't shop for groceries. Or can she?

Vygotsky suggested that there are pieces of any given task that are within a child's zone. Most three-year-olds know the names of common family food products. They may even know where they are located in the store. They can get bananas, even though they might be squished. And they can grab a roll of paper towels, even thought it might not be "Select-A-Size" with flower print on the edges.

For learning to occur, someone must share the next level of knowledge with the child. And the next level should not be too far beyond where the child is currently. Three-year-olds can be taught that eggs should be put in the cart gently or they will break. They can learn to recognize their brand of yogurt. They can learn that one doesn't eat food in the store, one buys food in the store. The trick is in recognizing what a child currently knows and what she might be able to learn next.

In Vygotsky's theory, the act of taking a child to the next level of knowledge is called "scaffolding." Scaffolds are temporary structures that are used as supports. It's a wonderful metaphor because it suggests that initially, a lot of support is needed to help a child complete a particular task. Eventually, little or no support is needed. At least for that task. A new scaffold can then be created as the child moves up to the next level in the zone and learns something new. Thus, optimal learning occurs when a child is presented with a problem that is just beyond her current abilities and when learning happens with someone who is more skilled.

Vygotsky's theory is amazingly powerful. The emphasis on someone who is "more skilled" provides a wide range of potential teachers – parents, community leaders, classroom instructors, or caring peers. Watch a gifted "teacher." In most cases, they are using Vygotsky's theory, even if they don't know it. Research has shown that Vygotsky's theory applies to all sorts of situations ranging from Guatemalans teaching their young daughters to weave to American parents teaching their adolescents how to make sense of media influences.

Because Vygotsky's theory has no stages, it can also be applied at all ages – from birth to death. With a little effort, you can find Vygotskyan teaching and learning all around you. Parents use it to teach children language, high schoolers use it to teach their grandparents how to use e-mail, and older siblings use it when they teach younger siblings how to get their parents to agree to a dubious request.

Vygotsky also places learning smack in the middle of the social environment. It is interaction with others that promotes learning. Clearly, learners can make new discoveries on their own. Vygotsky didn't discount this type of learning. He simply highlighted the sociocultural transmission of knowledge. He recognized that learning can, and does, occur in community. Thus, all communities are potential classrooms. And these communities promote more than social development. They also promote cognitive development.

At Hanger Hall, every day serves as an example of Vygotskyan teaching and learning. Every excursion, every lesson, and every ritual is intended to keep the girls in their zones of proximal development. The creation of a solid community (See Chapter 1) and the establishment of basic behavioral rules (Chapter 2) provide the firm foundation needed for optimal learning to occur. Because that community includes the students, the parents, and the teachers, learning occurs among and between all players. The curriculum – in all its varied forms – then moves the girls beyond their current physical, cognitive, and emotional level in a safe and caring environment. With small classes and a low student-teacher ratio, learning can be individualized. Scaffolds are constructed, used, and remodeled. Day after day. Week after week. Vygotsky would definitely approve.

Notes

1. Hackel, A., Kimball, L., and Mannes, M. Exploring understandings of young people's spiritual development around the world: Parent perspectives. The Center for Spiritual Development in Childhood and Adolescence. Retrieved October 21, 2008 from http:/www.spiritualdevelopmentcenter.org/Display.asp?Page=parents.

2. See, for example, Benson, P.L., Roehlkepartain, E.C., and Hong, K.L. (Eds.) (2008). *New Directions for Youth Development: Spiritual Development*. San Francisco:Wiley/Jossey-Bass or Roehlkepartain, E.C., King, P.E., Wagener, L.M., and Benson, P.L. (Eds.) (2006). *The Handbook of Spiritual Development in Childhood and Adolescence*. Thousand Oaks, CA:Sage.

3. Fowler, J.W. (1981). *Stages of Faith: The Psychology of Human Development and the Quest for Meaning*. San Francisco: Harper & Row.

4. Fowler also based his work on Lawrence Kohlberg's theory of moral development. Kohlberg's work also served as the foundation for Carol Gilligan's research (See Notes for Chapter 5).

5. CBS News Poll. (April 6-9, 2006). Retrieved October 21, 2008 from http://www.pollingreport.com/religion.htm.

6. FOX News/Opinion Dynamics Poll. (November 29-30, 2005). Retrieved October 21, 2008 from http://www.pollingreport.com/religion.htm.

7. Atkinson, R.C. and Shiffrin, R.M. (1968). Human memory: A proposed system and its

control processes. In K.W. Spence and J.T. Spence (Eds.), *The Psychology of Learning and Motivation: Volume 2. Advances in Research and Theory*. NY: Academic Press.

8. Craik, F.I.M. and Lockhart, R.S. (1972). Levels of processing: A framework for memory research. *Journal of Verbal Learning and Verbal Behavior*, 11, 671-684.

9. Vygotsky, L.S. (1978). *Mind in Society: The Development of Higher Mental Processes*. Cambridge, MA: Harvard University Press. Vygotsky actually died in 1934 at the age of 37, but it took several decades for his ideas to be translated and to reach English-speaking audiences.

Moving Forward (Theoretically Speaking)

- *Nine* -
EXPLORATION

The best thing about Hanger Hall, is… well, the trips! – 7th Grader

Middle-school girls are in the business of exploration. Always, inevitably and in every way imaginable, middle-school girls yearn to explore. Middle school girls are social explorers, cognitive explorers, emotional explorers, physical explorers. Whether they are even conscious of it or not, girls of middle school age are forever exploring and seeking to discover what's out there in the world and what's inside their quickly developing brains and bodies.

Now, explorers are a special breed. And, in our culture we like to recognize famous explorers. From Marco Polo to Neil Armstrong, our written history is populated with explorers, most of whom are regarded in some way as heroes. Think of whatever explorers you remember from school: Balboa, Daniel Boone and St. Brendan, Edmond Hilary, Henry Hudson, Zebulon Pike. Then, there was Sacagawea, the Shoshone Indian guide who led Lewis and Clark on their famous expedition and who really deserves most of the credit for enabling Lewis and Clark to make their "discoveries."

Don't you find it interesting that the only two women whose faces appear on U.S. currency are Sacagawea and Susan B. Anthony – each an explorer in her own right? Sacagawea, with Lewis and Clark and Susan B. Anthony, in her battle for women's right to vote. As a protagonist for suffrage, Ms Anthony explored just how free the United States really was, how much power a women could exert and as an exploring activist, opened up totally new paths for women and for democracy.

Of course, like Susan B. Anthony, explorers are not always about geography. Anyone who is involved in research is an explorer. Anyone actively trying to develop new ways of addressing a problem is an explorer. Writers and poets can be explorers, as can dancers, musicians, graphic artists and sculptors. Any successful business that can stay afloat for many years must have explorers on staff - astute business-minded folks who are constantly looking outside the box, watching for trends, analyzing the competition, studying the market. The R&D (research and development) department is one of the most vital departments for any business which operates in a competitive market. Explorers come in all shapes and sizes with all kinds of agendas. And middle-school girls, in particular, are explorers. They are explorers of life and of the changes in life.

The Nature of The Age

So what is it that makes an explorer an explorer?

• **Explorers are travelers by nature.** This is absolutely true for middle school explorers. These girls love to travel physically, mentally, socially and emotionally. Further on in this chapter, we will describe the Hanger Hall emphasis on travel and how this vital part of the curriculum stimulates growth and development in every area of a girl's life. The importance of travel cannot be overstated.

• **Explorers are adventurers and sometimes risk-takers.** And though this can drive parents and teachers crazy (and can sometimes be a hazard to health or happiness), it is important to know that adventure and risk-taking are an integral part of the developmental process, part of the necessary steps that must be taken for a girl to get a sense of boundaries and possibilities, both within and without. (See Chapter 7) Adventure and risk-taking are a vital part of the development of self-esteem and self-assurance. But getting there can be scary.

• **Explorers acknowledge that they do not know it all.** If we knew it all, of course, there would be no need to explore. Explorers are excited, therefore, to make discoveries: 1) to find new things they never knew existed; 2) to come upon new ideas which can trigger other new ideas; 3) to hit upon new ways of thinking - abstract reflection, logical reasoning, cultural consideration. (See Chapter 3) Curiosity in students is what every educator longs for. In that regard, middle school girls are an educator's dream. And if the educator is wise, she will find ways to tap into that curiosity rather than simply trying to pump her own information agenda into the burgeoning, young brain.

- **Explorers need guides and maps.** Even the most proficient explorer needs some help along the way. Lewis and Clark had Sacagawea, Robert Peary had Eskimos, Neil Armstrong had NASA and Ponce de Leon had the Spanish empire to help him. All explorers need folks along the way to help them find their way. All explorers need maps (or even scraps of maps) to help get them where they need to be. Not that explorers ever really know where they're headed. All they know is that - chances are - there is something out there worth finding. Which is precisely the story of middle school girls. Middle-school girls need parents and teachers along the way.

Note: along the way - not all the way - not every step of the way. When your middle school girl seems to be pushing away from you, she is. Count on it. That's the nature of an explorer. It's what she has to do. She doesn't want (or need) to stay in the harbor. But, at the same time, she needs your guidance. She needs whatever maps or scraps of maps that you can offer. She may not acknowledge that she needs guidance when you offer it. She may appear to totally reject it. But, more than likely, she will use your guidance in some way, at some time in her journey of exploration.

Exponential Learning and Thinking

Your middle-schooler's awareness of herself and life around her is expanding exponentially - literally, exponentially. Remember middle-school math? Remember exponents? Remember $(x + y)^3$? "3" is the exponent. $(x + y)^3$ means the sum total of whatever x and y might be, to the third power. And what does the third power mean? It means multiplied by itself three times. If $x + y = 2$. Then, 2, to the third power means $2 \times 2 \times 2 = 8$.

This is precisely how your middle-schooler's development is happening. No single developmental aspect in her blossoming life happens by itself. None of her changes happen in isolation. Each new development inevitably expands to the 3rd or 4th or 5th power, at least. Whether it's a physical change or emotional, mental or social, each change is multiplied by itself many times in different areas of her life.

In Chapter 6, hormones were described as "cell phones." Hormones are the ways that cells in the brain begin talking. Cells, which had never talked before, are now in communication, thanks to hormones. Hormones puts different parts of the brain in touch other parts of the brain. And then, the cells in these various parts of the brain begin to chatter with cells in still more remote parts of the brain. So what started as a single hormone-induced "cell-phone" communication, now involves hundreds of thousands of cells throughout the brain all yakking with each other - all firing synapses left and right and up and down and over and under, exponentially.

Exploring With the Abstract

One of the countless results of this cognitive cell communication is abstract thinking. In many chapters of this book, we discuss the subject of abstract thinking as a new ability that dawns in pubescence. The ability to think abstractly is, indeed, a huge leap in cognitive ability. All of a sudden, this 10-12 year-old girl who has spent most of her life up to this point thinking in concrete terms and tangible images, is now able to think abstractly and theoretically. She is now beginning to come to terms with the abstract ideas of beauty, happiness, horror, color, pathos, wisdom, lunacy without needing a specific concrete example. Not only can she describe something that is beautiful to her, for example, she can also relate to the suggestion of beauty, itself. She can then take that ephemeral concept of beauty and apply it to every area of her thinking. And this kind of exploration happens exponentially.

So, now, with that newly found, astounding ability to think abstractly, your middle-school girl can begin to bundle different bits of information together. All the buildings she sees or has ever seen, for example, now can be filed in her mental "architecture bundle" along with the awareness that there are people who make a living practicing architecture and that, in a very real sense, architecture is our world's most abundant and visible art form. Older buildings may trigger the awareness that architecture changes with the times. Styles of buildings in urban and rural areas or in different cities across the country may prompt an awareness of practicality and aesthetics. She is, in Vygotsky's terms, "in the zone." She is "scaffolding." (See Chapter 8)

With this budding abstract consciousness of architecture, buildings are no longer just buildings for the middle-schooler. People who design buildings are no longer just architects. Art is no longer just something that hangs on a wall. History now has a new dimension and geography has a new dynamic. The girl's cognitive attentiveness to buildings, structures, design, career, art, history, landscape, architecture and construction has leapt forward enormously and exponentially. She has become a true explorer.

Exploring with a Variety of Stimuli

So, as a parent or teacher, coach or group leader, you can nurture her seed of cognitive exploration by providing as much good soil and nutriment as possible. Books, magazines, videos, concerts, plays, board games (Yes, board games! Games like "Scrabble," "Taboo," "Apples and Oranges," "Scategories" and "Clue," for example, are all excellent games that are both fun and mentally stimulating.) Remember: cognitive stimulation doesn't have to be drab or boring. (See Chapter 10) In fact, the more fun it is, the more intriguing and motivating it becomes.

Educational games are popular with many teachers at all grade levels. At Hanger Hall the teachers often find or create games dealing with one academic pursuit or another. Humanities Jeopardy, Survival of the Fittest (a calorie game with popsicle sticks), Environmental Detective, etc. Not only do these games provide a welcome relief from desks, tables and chairs, the game-playing interaction with other students can be crucial in this cognitive exploration process. Keep in mind the exponential factor: every synapse stimulates other synapses. Interfacing laughter, chatter and physical activity with mental pursuits is a most excellent way of getting those cerebral cells talking to each other.

Several years ago, there was a big media hubbub about the "Mozart Effect." Dr. Alfred A. Tomatis, in his book, *Pourquoi Mozart?*, proposed that listening to the music of Mozart accentuated learning and promoted development of the brain. There were many educators - probably Mozart aficionados - who climbed on the bandwagon (so to speak) and began using the music of Mozart in their classrooms and recommended that parents play the music at home while the children studied. There were also, of course, detractors - some of whose studies showed very little difference between Mozart-enhanced learning and learning in silence.

Whether or not Mozart is the answer to brain development or not, Dr. Tomatis was absolutely correct in his assumption that one stimulus to the brain – be it music, art, physical activity, competition, laughter, discussion, media, travel or whatever - triggers other stimuli. Inevitably. Exponentially.

Exploring Social Connections

Friends are like fruit: you try to pick out the sweet ones. – Madi, grade 7

If you read Chapter One or if you have spent any time around middle school girls, you should be fully aware of how important connections are to girls of this age. Connections are for these girls – in a very real sense – a lifeline. Connections are anchors in the storm, handholds in the roller coaster. With all of the changes going on during this time, social connections are vital.

The Dreaded Sexual Exploration

So, your middle-school girl is extremely apt to be exploring all kinds of connections. And, of course, the social connection most parents (and perhaps teachers) worry about, is her exploration of sexual connections with boys and/or girls. Every parent knows that this exploration is normal. And nearly every parent freaks out about it.

Maybe that's because parents remember their own behavior during these years. Maybe, it's the awareness of STD's (not the least of which is AIDS), pregnancy, school reputation, self-esteem and just plain-old getting hurt. Whatever it is, when a middle school girl begins exploring her sexuality, it can threaten the daylights out of her parents.

From our experience at Hanger Hall, our collected wisdom from counselors and from the experience of the many parents who have talked with us over the years, a few basic and helpful understandings have surfaced:

A) **Relax and accept it.** It's going to happen, it's normal and there's nothing you can do to stop it. Sooner or later, the vast majority of middle school girls will find a way to explore their newfound sexuality. They might explore it with books, movies, pop songs or late-night discussions with friends. It doesn't necessarily mean that they will become sexually active in the physical realm. Your daughter may remain a virgin until she gets married. Your daughter may remain a virgin all her life. But you can bet that mentally and emotionally, sexual interest and (sometimes) activity kicks in during these years. Remember that no less than 150 years ago, it was ever-so common in this country for a 14 year-old girl to be married and having children. It's still true in other parts of our world today. Sexual thoughts, sexual fantasies, sexual feelings are normal. Natural, healthy and expected. Take a deep breath, Mom and Dad. It's OK.

B) **Parents and teachers are vital.** Simply because your daughter or your students are engaged in some very private matters, it doesn't mean that parents and teachers are helpless or useless. Not at all! This sexual exploration (like almost everything else during these years) is new stuff. It's familiar in the sense that it's all over the media; but as an integral part of life, sex is like a foreign language. You may recognize it as real; but you don't understand it. Therefore, it is vital that parents and teachers make themselves available to talk, to answer questions, to offer books or videos. It's important to let your daughters and students know that you know what they are going through, and that you will be there for them.

At Hanger Hall, we absolutely and totally believe in sex-education. But our "sex-ed" classes cover far more than how the reproductive system works. We talk about feelings. We talk about emotions. We talk about the importance of taking care - not just of your body, but of your heart, of your mind and of your sense of who you are. The physiological (how it works) piece is crucial, to be sure; and there are countless books and videos that can address that aspect of sexual development. Use them. Offer them. Your middle-school girl wants to be in the know. She doesn't want to be that last one on the block to catch on.

Yes, parents and teachers, you have a place in this process - a crucial place. You are absolutely essential during these precious years of sexual exploration and development. And your job is never to condemn, but to assist, to guide, to be there for these girls with information and love. (And a quick word to you Dads: Don't be upset if your daughter talks to her mom more than to you. This is a girl thing and a woman-to-woman matter. But you are still absolutely vital, Dad. You can be there with three of the things your daughter needs the most: hugs, acceptance and affirmation.)

C) **Deal with the media.** Yes, middle school girls are aware of sex. Yes, they have seen it in movies and television, books and magazines. They have heard it described, extolled and condemned in pop songs and late night discussion with friends. But that certainly doesn't mean they know everything they need to know or that they have seen it all. So where do you draw the line? How do you decide what is appropriate and what is not? At Hanger Hall, we do not operate with a laissez faire

– "whatever" – approach to the media. Nor do we ever think we can totally limit what our middle-school girls experience with the media. That will never happen. What we do is communicate with them. We let them know the kind of things that are out there. We talk about what denigrates women and sex and what shows women and sex in a good light. We let them know of the media representations of which we don't approve and we tell them why. But, we do our best to be open to their questions, responses and disagreements. We want our girls to know beyond the shadow of a doubt, that we are there for them and are fundamentally interested in their own healthy sexual development.

But, here's where the waters get choppy: one girl's parents may say it's fine for their daughter to go to a PG-13 or even an R-rated movie. You, as a teacher or parent, may disagree. So, you enter the battleground as she lays down the gauntlet with a, "She gets to go. Why can't I?" And, of course, there is no easy answer here. Did you actually think parenting and teaching were easy? As a teacher, of course, all you can do is to give your opinion. Decisions like that fall to Mom and Dad.

As parents, it's best, of course, for you to have seen the movie in question and decide for yourself. But that can't always happen. Finally, it is your role to make that call, knowing that your daughter is doing her best to do what she is made to do - to grow and develop into an emerging young woman. She is not an 8 year-old anymore. And whatever your decision about movies or television or internet or books or magazines, it is fundamental that you 1) deal with it and not try to sweep it under rug; 2) acknowledge that you and your daughter are growing and developing together. You can share things she needs to know; and she can share things you need to know about her.

Exploration with Friends

There are few things more vital in the life of a middle-school girl than friends. Listen in sometime on a gaggle of middle-school girls. They talk about everything. Make that EVERYTHING. And they talk non-stop. They sing, they laugh, they get petulant. They get animated, keyed up, energetic, effervescent. They play with each other's hair. They give each other make-overs. They snuggle together like piles of puppies and watch a movie or listen to a song.

At Group (a time when the entire School comes together for schedules, issues or discussion) the girls often sit in each other's laps, hold hands, lean against each other. Their connections as friends go far beyond the connections that boys have. A middle-school boy may care just as deeply for his friends, but, unless he is exploring a homosexual connection, he probably won't express that care in any physical touching. Most middle-school boys do not snuggle together, sit in each other's laps or play with each other's hair. Nor do they necessarily yabber non-stop. Twelve year-old boys might be quite content quietly playing video games together or roller-blading or shooting baskets. But this is not so with their female counter-parts.

Keep in mind that what a lot of the girl-chatter is about, is processing. Girls are dealing with feelings, thoughts, concerns, delights, worries, fears. Girls explore by chatting. They discover more about themselves by tossing out ideas and gauging the responses. When a bunch of middle-school girls get together, their obvious agenda is to have fun. But, their sub-conscious agenda, most assuredly is all about growth, development and exploration.

Loners

Now, admittedly, there are some girls who tend to be loners. At Hanger Hall, out of our annual student population of 70 or so, we see about one loner a year. What we call "loners" are simply girls who find ways to entertain themselves by themselves. Sometimes there are issues; but often the behavior doesn't necessarily appear to be unhealthy or anti-social. We have discovered that some girls are simply more quiet, shy, introspective and less gregarious, outgoing or communicative. Some girls take longer to reach out for friends. And some truly prefer to go it mostly alone. We do not push these girls toward any kind of friend connection. We do not assume that something is wrong with them. But we definitely let them know that there are girls in the School who would like to be their friends and that the teachers are always there for them.

We have found that nurture, affirmation and encouragement are far more effective tools in facilitating the maturation process than pushing, manipulating, controlling, or in any way trying to force things to happen. Just as you can't make a flower open, nor can you compel a middle-school girl to open. Flowers, like middle-school girls, have their own time schedule, their own pattern of growing, their own way expressing their beauty. And, we have found that when you take the pressure off and replace it with nurture, affirmation and encouragement, our "loners" find their way with grace and ease. Some begin to reach out for friends. Others settle in comfortably with being by themselves.

We have almost always had a few girls who read all the time. These voracious readers go through book after book, week after week. On field trips, these girls sit on the bus by themselves and immerse themselves in books while the girls around them are singing, laughing, hooting and hollering. Sometimes, of course, immersing yourself in a book is a way of hiding from the world around you. Sometimes, it can become a refuge for a girl who does not feel accepted by the group or is feeling sad or disconnected for some reason. Our teachers are constantly aware of these possibilities and are quick to talk with these girls, if they sense that something is wrong.

But, for most of these avid readers, it's all about the book. And the other girls learn swiftly to respect that and not to try and drag the reader into the conversations, songs and silliness. These readers seem ever-so comfortable doing what they were doing; and they serve as an example to the other girls that there are different strokes for different folks.

But even passionately reading loners need connections and will find connections that work for them. As parents and teachers, it is your job to find the line and then walk that line between allowing your middle-schooler the freedom to explore and express herself, and the openness to offering and being a connection for her.

Exploration with Adults

Your middle-schooler's world is expanding ever-so-obviously in some ways, and in other ways far more subtle and understated. For one thing, she is getting out into the world more often on her own or with her friends. She doesn't walk through the mall holding Mommy's hand, anymore. In fact, she tends to distance herself from Mom and Dad. And though, this can break a parent's heart and can set up all kinds of anxious moments, that distancing is part of the development and exploration process. A middle-school girl is preparing herself for the time when she will operate alone. And she needs practice. Remember, Mom and Dad: your job as parents is to work yourselves out of a job.

So, without Mom and Dad in tow, the middle-school girl discovers that she has to relate to adults without parental help. If she's shopping in the mall, for example, she must deal with the sales people and cashiers on her own. She can't (and won't) hide behind Mama's skirts and let Mama do the talking. She must relate to these unknown and unfamiliar adults by herself. If she's going over for a spend-the-night at a friend's house, she must relate to the friend's parents and any other adults who happen to be present. If she goes with friends to the movie, she must relate to the ticket and popcorn sellers and anyone else who happens to be at the theater. In short, as the result of her "coming of age," the middle school girl is quickly thrust into the presence of many new adults with whom she must learn to communicate.

In Chapter 7, we focused on social skills: eye contact, interest in the other person, etc. Learning and becoming comfortable with these social skills is one of the most important abilities that a middle-school girl can acquire. Practicing these skills can 1) ease the discomfort and anxiety that often comes in meeting new people; 2) offer a sense of confidence and self-assurance to the girl; 3) enable her to explore her new adult relationships with integrity, openness, poise and clear boundaries; 4) assist in developing her own maturity by relating to (hopefully) more mature people;

and 5) help establish clear boundaries for all involved. Teachers and parents can offer invaluable lessons and guidance in how to relate to adults. Being able to relate confidently is an absolutely essential skill for a middle school girl.

Exploring Physically

Her body is changing. It is dramatically changing. In just a few short years, a middle school girl will lose her little-girl body forever and develop her adult body, which will be with her for the duration of her life. This can be frightening, upsetting, exciting, stimulating, worrisome, embarrassing, thrilling and energizing all at the same time. Likewise, that wide range of emotions can show up on different days at different times with different people.

Some girls fret that their breasts have not developed like their friends. Some wish that their breasts had waited a bit to develop. Some can't wait for their menstruation to start. Others would rather put it off as long as possible. Some girls are chagrinned about having hair under their arms or on their legs and pubis. Others love the novelty and the feeling of being a real woman. Some girls lose baby fat during pubescence; some gain extra weight in the hips and thighs. Just like the cognitive and social development, the physical development for each girl is unique and distinctive. There are girls who start their period at age 10. Others wait until they are 15-16. There are girls who wear a C cup at age 12; others don't need a bra until they are 14.

But one thing is certain: By the time she finishes middle school, a girl will have a radically new body: new shape, new weight, new attributes and new abilities. By the time she finishes middle school, a girl will have an adult body. Young adult, to be sure, but an adult body nonetheless. By the time she finishes middle school, no one will ever again mistake her for a child. That is a massive shift. This is an enormous concept for the girl to get her mind and emotions around.

Like it or not, Mom and Dad, coming out of middle school, your daughter will be turning heads. No matter how attractive she is with her personality, wit and charm, she will now be attractive in the physical sense. She will be eye-catching; and she knows it.

Now, if ever there were a list of woman-to-woman issues, the female body would be right at - or very close to - the top. As a girl explores her budding adult body, it is vital that the women in her life offer all the help possible. Here again, pushiness almost always fails. But, support, encouragement, guidance, affirmation will win the day. At Hanger Hall, teachers feel free to interrupt an academic study session to address whatever personal issues come up. If these issues seem appropriate for class discussion, then the teacher can and will lead that discussion. And the teachers report that the talk can be about everything from deodorant to hair care to tampons to pregnancy to boys to drugs to sex scenes in the movies to embarrassing moments, etc, etc. – and almost every bit of the discussion often has, in some way, to do with the body.

Eating Disorders

It is during the middle-school years that some girls develop eating disorders. Bulimia anorexia binge eating are far too common in our world to be ignored. Some lay the blame for these disorders on our media portrayal of what we call "female beauty." Fashion models tend to be far below normal weight; and female movie- and rock-stars all seem to share the same body shape. Check out the cover of almost every woman's magazine and, chances are, you will see an article on how to lose weight.

On the other hand, there are those who feel that eating disorders are a way for a girl to have some sense of control over her life. As we have discussed in several chapters of this book, the middle-school years are up-to-their-eyeballs in enormous changes for girls. Physical, emotional, social, cognitive changes are exploding within each of these girls. So, for a girl to use eating and food to gain control over her life might just be a possibility.

One thing we know about eating disorders is that we do not know it all. But we do know that it's real. We do know that some girls experiment with it and then, let it go. We do know that some girls use gymnastics, sports, dancing and running to feel a sense of control. And we do know, that unfortunately, some girls do actually suffer with a life-threatening eating disorder.

At Hanger Hall, we are vigilant when it comes to signs of possible eating disorders; but, neither do we obsess over the possibility, nor do we freak-out if we think we detect it in our students. We talk about it in our media and sex-ed studies; but we do not focus on it. We do, however, communicate our concerns with parents and offer them references for help.

When it comes to a middle-school girl's exploration of her body, what it all boils down to is this: Whoever you are, if you work with middle-school girls, be there for them.

Transforming Travel

Traveling at Hanger Hall is like a fun-filled adventure. Also, it's like traveling with your family, except it's more fun because it's with all your friends. The difference between traveling with your parents or friends is that your friends aren't as embarrassing and your parents aren't as much fun. No offense, parents. - Katie, grade 7

At Hanger Hall, we are totally convinced of this: travel enhances learning and development. Travel enhances learning and development unbelievably, remarkably, extraordinarily, inevitably. Do we make our point clear?

The mission of Hanger Hall School is to nurture the girl and empower the emerging woman. From the day we opened the school, travel has been essential to the success of that mission. During her three years at Hanger Hall, we take a girl to a variety of safe places outside her comfort zone. We take her to places that she may not have been and put her in situations she may never have experienced. We keep her safe at all times and let her know repeatedly that she is protected.

But, outside the comfort zone (visiting different cultures, different geography, different living styles, different schedules) the girls in the School must find ways to deal with these differences and with the newness. It is made clear to all when we travel that we want the girls to deal with things they have never dealt with before. Which is, of course, precisely what they are doing on a day-to-day basis with their own personal development. So, travel becomes an outward expression of what is going on inside. Travel becomes a very tangible way of dealing with changes and transformations that mostly feel intangible. Travel puts in clear perspective the sensations, thoughts and emotions that mostly feel unclear.

We have regular, sometimes weekly, field trips to a variety of cultural and science-oriented venues. We also take the entire school to a camp for several days every year before classes begin. But, we also have our "big trips." For the past several years, we have taken our 6th graders to Charleston, SC. We stay right on a beautiful and safe beach where we can play and swim at night under the stars. During our days in Charleston, we take a boat trip to a barrier island with an ecologist to explore undisturbed nature. We see turtles' nests, bogs, snails, all kinds of birds, flora and fauna, most of which these mountain girls have never experienced. We take a tour of historic Charleston and have photo scavenger hunts of architectural detail. We visit Patriot's Point and the Maritime Museum. We go to historic churches and invite the girls to sketch a picture or write a poem. We go to the aquarium, the Imax, the open market. We go sea kayaking and visit plantation ruins.

And, at the end of the day, we ask the girls to do some journaling about what they've seen, what they've felt and what new things they have learned about Charleston and about themselves. If we're not too tired, we sometimes share these discoveries together in Group, remembering that, in the sharing we are hopefully helping these girls learn to process all the information that is flowing into their lives and within their lives.

If you hate something, get good at it. - Grace, grade 7

Learning to Live Outside the Comfort Zone & Deal With the Unexpected

Life is what happens after you've made your plans. It's not just a bumper sticker. It's true. We all know that. Control freaks naturally have a problem with it; but most everyone knows that that's the way it works. So, if we are in the business of nurturing, educating and motivating middle-school girls into successful adulthood, it behooves us to give these girls the tools that need live outside the comfort zone and deal with the unexpected.

Outward Bound is a national organization which offers young people the opportunity to learn how to survive in the wilderness. Their mission is, in part, "to inspire character development and self-discovery…through challenge and adventure and to impel (all persons) to achieve more than they ever thought possible." And the way Outward Bound follows through and fulfills this impressive mission, is to take these kids out of their comfort zone and force them to deal with things they might never have encountered before.

What Outward Bound succeeds in accomplishing is what each parent and teacher should seek to accomplish, as well. It is of the highest importance for middle-school girls to 1) realize that life doesn't always turn out the way you want or expect it to; 2) have the emotional, social, physical and cognitive tools to deal with life when it veers off in a different direction than you had hoped for or anticipated.

Making explorers out of your middle-school girls is one of the best ways of offering tools for dealing with the unexpected, and enabling them to discover remarkable abilities they already have within. And why is this?

- Explorers know that there is always more out there than we have seen.
- Explorers know that danger and frightening experiences are part of the story.

- Explorers know that there are astonishing treasures to be discovered.
- Explorers know that you always need to ask for help along the way.
- Explorers know that each day is a brand new adventure.

Some folks try to move through life as tourists. They want to have reservations, tour guides, interpreters. They want to have each and every detail planned out. They want nothing to go wrong. They want never to lose their luggage or be inconvenienced in any way.

Now, that may work for short trips abroad; but it doesn't work on the big trip through life. Never. Not ever. So, teaching your kids to live as explorers in their lives rather than tourists, can be one of the finest and longest-lasting gifts your can offer.

Four Easy Pieces

So, how do we do move them from being tourists to explorers? There are many, many ways. Enrolling them in Outward Bound is a grand start. But, there are things you can do on a daily basis that can kick in the explorer genes.

1) Teach and play the simple game called, "Now What?" It's a game that can be played at almost any moment of the day; but it's often best played at the pivotal moments. The rules are simple. At any time, you simply stop what you're doing and ask the question, "Now What?" And then, you list at least three possibilities of actual things you can do to get yourself where you want to be. That's the key: To get yourself to the next step toward where you want to be.

For example:

a) You fail a test. Now, what?

b) You win a race. Now, what?

c) You break your leg. Now, what?

d) Some attractive someone has been paying attention to you. Now, what?

You get the idea. And, of course, it's important to remember and remind your middle-schooler that there are people all around who might be able to come up with even more answers to your own "Now What?" That's what doctors, counselors, ministers, friends – not mention teacher and parents – are for.

2) Read: particularly fiction and biographies. The most interesting biographies, of course, are the ones whose main character faces the most challenges. Likewise, with fiction, remind your girls that no one likes a story in which everything goes well for the hero or heroine. A really good story involves life-threatening situations and terrifying possibilities. Being able to see how other people (actual or fictional) dealt with their adversity can be an enormous inspiration and stimulation for any would-be explorer. And then, a classroom or one-on-one discussion of these heroes and heroines can bring to light all kinds of ways that life outside the comfort zone can be faced.

3) Talk. Or, more to the point, reflect, as in, guided reflection. You get a group of 11, 12, 13 year-old girls together – preferably those who have spent some time together, and there will be chatter - lots of chatter. And much of the chatter has to do with, "What I like," or "What we did," or "What she did," or "That's so gross," or "That's so cool." One way or another, they are reflecting. So, as a parent or teacher, you can find a way to guide a reflection time by asking certain questions.

You might say, for example, "For the next ten minutes, we want you to reflect on something that didn't go like you planned it and how you dealt with it." Then, look out! If you're not a strong leader, you'll never shut them off in 10 minutes. And the beauty of this kind of reflection is that it allows each girl to talk about her challenges and allows each girl to hear how others dealt with their challenges. It's a fine way for explorers to learn from one other.

4) Do some exploring on your own. As parent or teacher, you know your middle-school girls as well as anyone. So, do a little exploring in your own creative bag. Find things that have worked for you in the past: How did you get through your divorce? How did you deal with losing your job? What did you do after the car wreck? How did you quit smoking? Or what are you doing to try? What has inspired you to get through the hard times? What has punched your motivation button? What has enabled you to keep on keeping on? You have been at this life thing much longer than your middle-school kids. You have a deeper bag of tricks at your disposal. Use them!

Allowing Her to (Sometimes) Lead the Way

Middle-school kids have not been at this life thing very long. It's true. But, on the flip side, these kids have a more-fresh and less-jaded view of the world. They can see things that you either can't see or things you have forgotten about.

Middle school girls are astounding creatures. Part-child, part-adult, these remarkable beings surge through life brimming with childhood enthusiasm and semi-adult points of view. They can articulate feelings and emotions that they couldn't just a few years ago. They can describe abstract concepts that would have felt utterly foreign to them just awhile back. They can wrap their young, fertile minds around ideas and events, history or mathematical formulas and offer unsullied and brand spanking new observations.

This won't last forever. It's a precious moment in time. So, as a teacher, parent, coach, group leader – however you work with these girls – your job is to not let this amazing time slip by. Whatever you do, treasure this unreservedly unique instance and allow yourself to receive the gifts that these girls have to offer. These remarkable beings can lead you to new discoveries about the world and about yourself. They can remind you of things you had forgotten - important things. They can even help you get your life back on track, if you let them.

Do they know it all? No, although they might act like they do. But they do have a magical sense of things that adults often miss or ignore. They do have a way of seeing the world that can restore our faith in what might be. Teachers, parents and leaders of middle-school girls have an incredible opportunity to join in a life-giving dance of discovery and wonder during these middle-school years – these years that are, indeed, a most precious window of time.

- Ten -
ACADEMICS

I have always been pretty loud and talkative but now I feel as if my voice matters. I know my voice matters. It has taken me a while to realize it but I feel smart. I know I am smart. – Darian, Grade 8

If you have been reading this book from front to back, you have probably been asking yourself, "OK, when do we get to the academics? Isn't that what school is really all about?" And, the answer is, "Yes." And the answer is, "No."

The word, academic, comes from the Greek, *akademeia*, as in, The Grove of Akademos. Akademos is a legendary Athenian whose estate near Athens, Greece, was the place where Plato led his school sometime around 350-400 BCE. Keep in mind that for Plato, education was not just about reading, writing and arithmetic. Nor did Plato have any truck with standardized tests. For Plato, education included everything from the way you speak to the way you think to the way you act. The study of literature was just as important to Plato as the study of virtue or art or philosophy or the nature of knowledge, itself. Plato's "Academy of Athens" was, as far as we know, the first place of formal "higher education" in Western Civilization. And it was a place where virtually all of life was observed, examined and scrutinized. And it is from this place, teacher and tradition that we get our word, academic.

Be that as it may, the word, academic, has now come to mean scholarly performance or higher learning. Academic subjects include everything from math to history to science to philosophy to language arts. Academic subjects do not traditionally include art, music or dance if actual practice or performance is involved. Though there might be an academic course titled, "The History of Art, Music and Dance," traditionally, the students in that class would not be painting, playing or dancing. Likewise, academic subjects do not traditionally involved technical or vocational education. If you're learning a trade, it's not conventionally considered an academic pursuit. Some might define academic subjects as those subjects which appear to have no practical purpose or use.

Q: What's the main question a liberal arts university graduate asks?
A: "You want fries with that?"

We know that's not true, of course. Academics are often tied in closely with career. The study of organic chemistry is crucial if you want to become a doctor. Likewise, you may need many courses in higher math (algebra, calculus, fractals, statistics & probability) if you intend to work as an engineer or nuclear physicist. And, if you're going to become a middle school history or humanities teacher, you'd best plan to study everything from ancient history to archaeology to anthropology.

The Creative Mix

What we're saying here is that it's all academics. Every aspect of education is somehow linked to every other piece. Everything connects with everything else. And one of the best things teachers and parents can do for a middle school girl, is to help her see how they are all connected. "I'll never use algebra in my daily life," moans your 8th grader as she studies for a big test. "Why am I doing this?" And, on the one hand, she may be right. She may never use algebra, per se, as part of her career or daily life style. But, if she can come to see that the study of algebra expands her mind in ways that nothing else can… if she can come to realize that none of us – not a single one – knows exactly what our lives will be like in 5-10 or 15 years; and that the best way to deal with the unknown is to be ready for anything or as much of anything as is possible, then she might come to appreciate algebra a bit more. If you can help her see that having some algebraic skills in her bag of tricks just might make all the difference, you will have offered her at least the possibility of a purpose for all her work. When we can understand the why of things, we can often endure almost any how.

Multi-disciplinary education has been a buzzword in academic circles for a long time. The idea of relating one subject to another so that the student can find continuity between the two has been a popular theme in many schools. If a student is studying the history of the French Revolution, for example, she might be introduced simultaneously to the art, music, drama and literature of late 18th and early 19th century.

She could listen to French Revolution contemporaries, Haydn, Beethoven or Mozart who died in 1791. She might eat some Camembert cheese, which was invented in the same year. Or she might listen to "La Marseillaise" (the French national anthem), which was composed around the same time. She could pass around a sprig of absinthe or talk about French chemist, Pierre Ordinaire, who, in 1792, used the herb to create a tonic, which later became an alcoholic drink. Or, she could discuss the discovery of the head of a giant dinosaur (later named Mosasaurus) which Napoleon's army found in the 1780's and brought back to France. She might pass around and taste ketchup, which was invented in Massachusetts in 1795, or sip a little lime juice which was proposed by Captain James Cook as a defense against scurvy, and subsequently issued to all British sailors in 1795. So many concurrent events with the French Revolution, so little time.

Now, on the one hand, exploring all these seemingly random incidents and discoveries may not help your students remember the year Marie Antoinette was beheaded or when Napoleon installed himself in France as the First Consul. But it might. And you can, in the meantime, be sure that these seemingly haphazard connections to the time of the French Revolution will heighten your students' interest, create animated classroom conversation and very possibly trigger some creative ideas in some 12 and 13 year-old brains.

At Hanger Hall, we encourage our teachers to share lesson plans with each other on a weekly and sometimes daily basis. Simply knowing even a bit about what the other teachers are teaching can open all kinds of connecting doors and windows and allow fresh and invigorating ideas to blow through. And we find that, not only do students benefit by this pedagogical overlapping, the teachers get an extra edge, as well. One idea invariably leads to another and before you know it, your lesson plan has expanded and opened up in ways you might never have thought possible on your own.

The Basics

So what are the academic subjects that a middle school girl needs to learn? The possibilities are mind-boggling, of course; and no one can honestly lay claim to the final answer. At Hanger Hall, we start with the prescribed curriculum by the North Carolina Department of Education. That way, we know that our girls will, at the very least, be up to speed with the girls from the rest of the State. But, for Hanger Hall, the State-designated courses are our base line.

Our "core curriculum" consists of math (pre-algebra, algebra, geometry), science (chemistry, physics, environmental studies, biology), humanities (history - ancient to modern, literature), language arts (grammar, syntax, expository writing, public speaking), foreign languages (French, Spanish), art, drama and music. Every student, every year, studies each of these disciplines.

Hanger Hall is all about building foundations - academic & personal foundations. We want our students to move into high school with a solid grounding in what might be called "classical education."

In the early universities, there was a popular pattern of education called the trivium. A Latin word, meaning "three ways," the trivium consisted of grammar, logic and rhetoric. Grammar was for the younger students. The Grammar phase was all about learning the basics: facts, language rules, history, science. The Logic phase was when you began to start putting the facts together: how one thing affects another. Why things work and why they don't. The Rhetoric phase was about expressing what you had learned through writing and speaking along with expressing your own developing interests in further study. Grammar, Logic, Rhetoric. At Hanger Hall, we try to cover all three.

We want never to assume that a child from elementary school has gotten the grounding she needs with facts, language rules, history and science. We want to be sure that her "grammatical bases" are covered. Likewise, with the Logic and Rhetoric phases. We do all we can to make certain that when our students enter high school, they will be as well prepared as they can be with foundational learning.

At the same time, of course, we are doing all we can to enable these young emerging women to secure a firm footing with their social, emotional and physical selves. And, though personal and academic foundational work may sound like an enormous challenge, the good news is that nature is working with you. A middle school girl's brain and body are ready receptors to this kind of development and growth. They are actively seeking grounding. They are vigorously in search of ways and means to establish a sense of self - a sensation of identity and an awareness of who they are and who they becoming. Solidly grounding academics under-girds that priceless pursuit.

Active Learning

Cross training is part of most athletes' workout schedules. If you're a runner, for example, cross training means you don't just run every day. Some days, you might work with weights or play soccer. You might go skiing or swim laps. You might do some yoga, pilates or tai chi. The idea behind cross-training is that your body is a total working unit. Every muscle, bone and tendon depends on every other muscle, bone and tendon. And even though the act of running uses mostly certain muscle groups and not the others, those very muscle groups are connected to all the others. So, if all the non-running others are in shape, the chances are better that performance will be improved.

But, cross training has other benefits as well: 1) it conditions the entire body, 2) allows for flexibility and variety in training and 3) lessens boredom. Cross training is good for the whole body and mind. Have you ever said that you're going for a walk or bicycle ride to "clear your mind?" Have you ever wondered if going out dancing actually elicits a chemical response in the brain which makes you feel better? Certainly you're aware that a session of love-making can change your way of thinking. We know that certain activities trigger certain parts of the brain; so when the body moves in a wide variety of ways, you can be pretty certain that the brain will be activated in a wide variety of ways as well.

Academic cross training is equally effective. Not only do multi-disciplinary studies engage more areas of our brains, but physical activity in conjunction with learning can definitely generate new cognitive synapses and enhance the entire experience of learning. Just like the so-called "Mozart effect," we discussed in Chapter 9, (in which listening to Mozart was said to activate the learning centers of the brain), physical stimulus can augment the scholarship process immeasurably.

When you include physical activity as part of the learning process, you are doing a kind of cross training - mental/physical cross training. Like an athlete's cross training, the cognitive benefits are similar: 1) it conditions far more of the mind than simply sitting in a desk might do; 2) it allows for flexibility and variety in the thinking process; 3) (and this is a big one for middle-school girls) it virtually eliminates boredom.

Aware of the value of physical movement in cognitive development, our teachers at Hanger Hall regularly include bodily activity in class. There are so many examples of this active teaching model at Hanger Hall, an entire chapter could well be devoted to just that. Some examples of the body/mind cross training are:

In studying Michelangelo and the Sistine Chapel, students tape large sheets of drawing paper under the tables in the room and then crawl under the tables with art supplies; and while lying on their backs, paint scenes replicating the ceiling of the Sistine Chapel. (The results win no awards, but produce lots of laughter.)

One class acts out short (5 minute) scenes from Shakespeare's, "The Tempest." The class prepares a scene, goes out into one of the halls of the school building, rings a gong; and any teacher in any classroom on the hall has the option of letting her students out to be the audience for the 5 minute scene. There is always an audience.

In order to encourage and facilitate seminar-type discussion, one teacher has the students in her class become a machine. One student, standing, sitting or lying in place begins making some kind of motion with her body. The next stands, sits or lies down next to her and creates a complimentary motion. The two continue with the same motion. The next follows suit until the entire class becomes a machine working together.

In order to teach projection, our drama teacher takes her students outside, divides them into two lines facing each other about ten feet apart. Then, each one is given a line from a play they are studying. Each student delivers the line to the students opposite; and those students let the others know whether or not they were heard and understood. After both groups of students have delivered their lines, they all step back a few feet from each other and deliver another line. They continue to do this until they are, perhaps, fifty feet apart. The teacher reminds them that they cannot shout or scream; but they must project in way to he heard and understood clearly.

Our science teacher invites her students to do "The Atom Dance." After studying how atoms move in different elements, she has them perform an improvised dance as if they were atoms of solids, liquids or gas. She may divide the class into three groups (solids, liquids, gas) and have each group come up with their own choreography, which they present to the other "atoms."

Our French teacher regularly organizes French "protests." The class decides what they want to protest (not enough play time, too many tests, too few field trips, etc.) The students make signs in French, study what slogans in French they want to shout; and then, the French teacher, having received permission from the other teachers, goes from class to class "protesting." The students to whom they protest are asked to guess what they are protesting, whether they have studied French or not.

Our Spanish teacher often has the students play "Family Feud," all in Spanish. She also encourages Spanish fashion shows in which the girls get to dress up and then, in Spanish, describe their "fashionable" clothes to the rest of the students. Likewise, this teacher will bring in a variety of tasty snack foods; and, as the students figure out how to describe these foods and their ingredients in Spanish, they get to eat them.

In our annual Grammar-a-thon, the girls are taken outside and divided into several teams. The teams line up single file behind the starting line. Fifty feet away are several baskets, each of which is labeled either "Noun," "Pronoun," "Verb," "Adjective," "Adverb," "Proposition," "Conjunction," "Interjection," with a teacher standing behind. In front of each line of students is a stack or word cards. After a, "Ready, set, go!" the first girls in the teams pick up a card and race to the baskets while trying to decide what part of speech the word might be. They drop the card in the basket and then run back to the start line. When they arrive the next girl picks up a card and does the same. The teacher behind the baskets check to see if they dropped the word in the right basket. Then, at the end, the score is added up and a winner is declared.

If one teacher senses boredom, monotony and tedium in the class, she has them all get up and run a lap around the parking lot. (It's not a big parking lot and the teacher runs with them.) This teacher reports that almost every time she does this, the spirit of the class picks up after the run, and the sensation of tired dullness disappears.

One humanities class acts out Greek and Roman myths and sometimes has "Mythological Feasts" in which they cook and/or bring "Foods of the Gods" to be shared with other class members as part of whatever myth they are studying at the time.

Our art teacher sometimes has the students painting "Pastry Still Life," for which, she places doughnuts, éclairs, brownies, pies, croissants, tarts, quiches, etc on a table surrounded by the students. Once they have completed their still life, they devour the pastries while checking out and critiquing the other students' work.

These active-learning or academic cross-training examples are just the tip of the iceberg at Hanger Hall. We have discovered again and again the direct relationship between active minds and active bodies. Academic cross training.

Reflective Learning

Just as important as physical activity can be for cognitive development and the learning process, quiet reflection can pump the assimilation and integration factor to record levels. Middle school girls love to be active. And they love to be quiet. We discuss reflection in practically every chapter with this book and there is good reason for this: middle-school girls are dazzling reflectors. They are not only good at it, but they are eager to explore all the different avenues of reflection. Reflection is a way of cleaning up and tidying the brain so that new material can find a place.

Keep in mind that girls between the ages of 10-14 are developing new cognitive abilities faster than they can mess up their bedroom. Not only are their social connections and emotional facets flowering like a field of poppies, their brains are firing synapses in ways they have never experienced before. It's all new. And, in their exploration of that newness going on right inside their brains, remarkable discoveries are made. Reflection opens that world.

Middle-school girls love themes, especially themes which have to do with their daily lives - their goofs and glories, their hopes and dreams, their fantasies and fears. Give a group of these girls a theme on which to reflect, coupled with a suggested mode of reflection and then stand back. Girls of this age are constantly stirring their life's stew and most of the tasty (and not so tasty) morsels are almost always floating to the surface.

In humanities classes at Hanger Hall, novels, plays and historical stories are often explored by the girls in reflecting on "how I would feel if I were in (say) Anne Boleyn's shoes," or "if I were van Gogh and not able to sell my paintings," or "if I ever felt like Puck from 'Midsummer Night's Dream' had ever messed with my life."

In science classes, students are sometimes asked to reflect on (and document) personal water usage as a way of way understanding the demand-for and availability-of for clean water. Likewise, in the study of famous scientists, students are asked to reflect on their own thinking processes and personalities and find the similarities between themselves and (say) Isaac Newton, Galileo or Darwin. In studying Einstein's work with conservation and mass, students reflect on how creation comes into being: are babies (for example) actually brand new or simply recycled from other materials? And then, of course, when the human reproductive system is studied, the students can reflect for hours on end about love, marriage, babies and their own families.

You sometimes hear middle-school girls being referred to as "drama queens." And, certainly, many girls of this age deserve the title. A drama queen is one who can take even the most insignificant events in her day and make a drama out of it. If, for example, a teacher at school came down hard on the students for whatever reason, the middle-schooler's after-school description of the teacher's voice and actions might sound like a portrayal of Genghis Khan. Or, if another student at school was snippy or grouchy, hearing a later portrayal of the crabby one might have you conjuring images of Cinderella's step sisters. Any parents who have grounded their daughter for misbehavior may well have been treated to an impassioned treatise on the injustice and discrimination inherent in the punishment, and how none of her friends would EVER be punished by their parents for a similar misdemeanor.

It is important to keep in mind, however, that being a "drama queen" is one way of playing out and reflecting what's going on in her young psyche. Remember, this is new stuff to a middle-school girl. New social and emotional waves are crashing on her childlike shore; and playing out her life to friends and family - even in exaggerated terms – is one way of processing and reflecting on these new experiences, sensations and feelings.

When teen-aged boy and girlfriends break up, it can feel like the end of the world to the broken-hearted teen. And it doesn't help very much for a kind-hearted adult to offer the well-worn advice of, "Don't worry. There are a lot more fish in the sea." Teen-agers don't know that yet. They haven't learned it from within. They haven't lived through several break-ups, heartaches and disappointments. This is a brand new experience for them; and as far as they know, as badly as it hurts, this could well mark the end of the world as they know it. Weeping and wailing over hard times is yet another form of reflection, and should not be discouraged by parents or teachers. When sadness and sorrow happen, the best you can offer are your arms, your shoulder and your listening ear. Compassion is a far better healing agent than advice. Always. All ways.

So what does all this emotional reflection have to do with academics? Everything. Everything is part of it; and when a middle-school girl is given permission – or even encouraged – to reflect, it is one of the best ways to clear the mind and emotions, and lay out the welcome mat for academic learning and reflection.

Raising the Bar

The same middle-school girl who loves to reflect on her thoughts and feelings, past and present, also loves to look to the future. Hopes and dreams are easy discussion topics. And right along with their fascination with what might be, middle school girls appreciate being academically challenged. They are almost always pleased that someone thinks enough of them to confront their learning skills with a, "let's see if you can take on this advanced idea." Presented in a positive "you can do it" way, a challenge becomes a true compliment. Middle-school girls appreciate the fact that their teachers think they are capable of more.

Now, of course, good teachers know that the best way to alienate a student is to try to jump her too far ahead too soon. It a pedagogical premise that all students learn best one step at a time. Vygotsky (See Chapter 8) called it "scaffolding." The idea is that, for any new information to be fully understood and assimilated, there must be a foundation for the new knowledge. There must be a strong scaffold built one bar at a time, but always raising the bar. Vygotsky may have been was more concerned with scaffolding in regard to development; but in cognitive or academic arenas, the same notion applies.

Graduates of Hanger Hall tell us again and again how much of the material they study in high school is information and ideas they had studied at Hanger Hall. They tell us that they feel ever-so prepared in so many of their high school honors classes because of the background study they had already done in 6th, 7th and 8th grade. Nor do we get any feedback that our "teaching ahead" (as it's sometimes called) hinders any future curiosity or academic pursuit. Knowing that they were capable of much more in middle school tends to give these students the sense that they are capable of much more as they grow older.

The teachers at Hanger Hall are convinced that most middle school girls are capable of much more academic growth than our public school systems acknowledge. Part of our 6th grade curriculum, of course, involves a leveling of the academic playing field while acknowledging and enhancing students' individual strengths. Girls come to us from many different schools (including home schools) and, therefore, from many different teaching styles and approaches to learning. Some girls, for example, show up in our 6th grade without having learned their multiplication tables, but are highly conversant on the U.S. Civil War. Other new students are not sure of the difference between a noun and a verb, but are quite comfortable working with fractions. So, it takes awhile to learn who is strong in what areas, and then get everybody up to speed. But, once that happens, we have discovered that the students are more than ready to be challenged.

Nor do we load our students up with huge homework assignments. We are always and forever trying to find the balance between challenging academics and kick-back fun. But we are quite convinced that one of the best ways to keep a class excited about any particular subject is to raise the bar, and to let the students know that the bar has been raised - to let each girl know that we are entirely sure that she is competent and capable of far greater things than she might ever imagine.

What Does it Mean to Be Smart?

One vast disservice that we do to schoolchildren across the United States is to foster the equation: Good test scores = Smart students. With this pitifully shallow understanding of what quality education means, we then assume that high EOG scores means a great school; or a perfect SAT means a perfectly-education person. In many public school systems, we even base our teachers' pay on the test scores of the students in their classes.

Indeed, test scores are one way of determining how much information and critical thinking skills a student has amassed in her brain. Test scores can also be a fine measure of how capable a student is in test taking or how proficient she is in test taking on a particular day. But to claim that education can be totally evaluated in three hours with a #2 pencil is shamefully blatant reductionism.

Looking back on just the last 100 years, we find case after case of brilliant and talented people who failed-in and/or dropped-out-of school but were highly successful in their lives and careers. Rosa Parks, Peter Jennings, Richard Branson, Sean Connery, Carl Sandburg, Sonny Bono, Jimi Hendrix, Jimmy Dean, Louis Armstrong, Bill Cosby, Steven Spielburg and Henry Ford are but a few of those who didn't (or couldn't) make it in school, but who made vast contributions to our world. Of course, you can argue that the number of non-successful drop out students far surpasses the Bill Cosby's and Rosa Parks; but the fact remains that there are many different kinds of intelligences which standardized test scores cannot detect.

Yes, "smart" does mean well-read and well-taught and well-immersed in a wide variety of subjects. But the ability to store and spew facts or information is only one part of "smart," and arguably, not the even close to the most important.

The Study and Living of Life in its Fullness

Plato had it right. Academia is, finally, the study of life. All of life. It's the study of how life operates and how we can operate in it. If we teachers, parents, group leaders and coaches are doing our jobs, we are guiding these astounding cusp-riding girl-women into a vastly deeper and delightful experience of living. What we want for ourselves in this life, we must offer these vibrant young charges of ours. We must always and forever continue to discover new ways of opening these middle-school girls to the wonders that they are, the possibilities that they hold and the fullness of life that is there for each and all. This precious window of time will never be repeated; and what moves through that tiny window will affect everything. What happens during this precious time truly can make all the difference - not only in her world, but in all of creation.

POSTSCRIPT

I'm a Dad. That's how this story began and how it ends. I am a Dad who has been deeply enthralled and enchanted watching my daughters get on with their lives and having the gloriously challenging opportunity to participate in that process. It has been - and continues to be a non-stop, ever-changing kaleidoscope of dazzle and danger, glory and goof, wonder and wackiness, sorrow, sensation and surprise. The experience of being a father has inestimably broadened my experience of being a human. I will live all my days as a grateful man, grateful for the astounding gift of being a Dad.

What this ineffable and irreplaceable gift has triggered in me is a profound desire to offer every girl the prospect of growing and developing into a strong, capable, happy and fulfilled woman. My time and energy in these past few years has been devoted through Hanger Hall, to nurturing the girl and empowering the emerging woman. My hope is that this kind of focus and effort will not only enhance the lives of many women, but will, inevitably make this world a better place.

Our long-time patriarchal society has blatantly disregarded and disempowered women. Even here in our "land of the free and the home of the brave," it wasn't until 1920 that women were even given the chance to vote. The first congressional proposal for women's suffrage came in 1878; and it took 42 years of continuous struggle to finally pass the 19th amendment in which women were – for the first time – regarded as full United States citizens. It has been less than 100 years that women in this country have had a voice in their government!

The so-called "glass ceiling" has been opened up in a few places; but the process has been painfully slow. It wasn't until 2007, that Harvard University inaugurated Dr.

Drew Faust as the first woman president; and according to "Fortune Magazine," in 2008, only twelve of the Fortune 500 companies were run by women and only 24 of these companies had women in the top job. And, as of 2008, the United States has never had a woman president, nor even had one nominated for the post.

Today, like it or not, women are still in many ways, second-place citizens. They are quite frankly disallowed from all the rights and privileges of men. As the father of two incredibly talented and competent young women, I am simultaneously saddened and challenged by this barefaced and deliberate inequality. That's why Hanger Hall School exists and why this book is written.

It the fervent hope of Dr. Vicki Garlock and me, that this book will inspire educators, parents, coaches, church officials, dance instructors, music teachers, group leaders –all who work with middle-school girls – to find more and more ways to "nurture the girl and empower the emerging woman." It is our passionate dream to awaken in our culture an awareness of the life-changing gifts that these girls offer on a daily basis –gifts they can offer to a struggling, suffering and confused world.

With that said, I offer just a few little suggestions as a close to this book:
1) **Lighten up.** As important as teaching and nurturing middle-school girls may be, it is absolutely vital to keep a sense of delight alive. Laughter heals. Joy rejuvenates. Jazz trumpeter, Maynard Ferguson, used to say, "Music is far too important for me to take it seriously." Good advice in the profoundly important task of teaching and nurturing our young.
2) **Teach and nurture yourself.** A bored and burned-out parent or teacher not only has little to offer the young, but can actually impart a message that says: this is what adults become… this is what you have to look forward to. It is crucially imperative that if you are going to teach and nurture, you must learn and be nurtured on a regular basis. You know what works for you. Do it!
3) **Play with these kids.** No matter what your role with middle-school girls, you will do yourself and your charges an enormous favor by playing together – really

playing together with no lesson plan or ethical instruction in mind. Middle school girls are fun! Play board games, swimming games, ball games, mental games. Jump on a trampoline, play tennis or badminton, rummy or black jack, have a race or a climbing contest. The more you play with these kids, the more lighthearted and proficient you will become. I guarantee it.

4) Never stop dancing. It's all a dance, you know. Every particle of creation is in motion at the sub-atomic level; and every step of our lives is a step in The Dance. You can see your life and your work in many ways, of course. But, what if you viewed your life as a dance? And what if your job is simply, to listen for the beat - for the rhythm - and then move to that beat as best you can. The beat can come from birdsong, sunrise, taste of a blueberry or a magical dream. The beat can come from faith and fear, from laughter and tears, from memories and hopes, from successes and failures. Each of us hears the beat in his or her own way. Then, all we need do is to move with it and to share that dance with our middle-school girls so that they can learn to dance into adulthood. In every dance, of course, no matter what it is, you will eventually stumble or step on toes. You'll embarrass yourself or fall flat on your face. But it doesn't matter, because we all do it, sooner or later. We all stumble and bumble. We all trip the light fantastic. But one way or the other, each and every one of us is part of that grand and goofy, sorrow and joy-filled dance of Life. Dance on!

APPENDIX

Seven Arenas of Change and Growth

Every change, of course, affects everything else. Quantum mechanics has taught us that. Even the simplest change. Changing your shoes, for example, can affect the way you walk which can affect the way you feel which can affect the way you interact which can affect your outlook which can affect your study habits which can affect your grades which can affect your self-esteem, and on and on. Just changing your shoes!

So imagine how a change in your body shape and function, in the way your mind processes ideas, in the way people relate to you… imagine how pervasive and forceful these changes can be! This kind of all-encompassing change is precisely what every middle-schooler is experiencing every day.

As we have said it over and over, for middle-schoolers. change is the name of the game - change and transformation. The teachers at Hanger Hall School are constantly amazed by how quickly and dramatically our students change. Everything from moods to hairstyles to friends to musical tastes… from favorite subject in school to favorite movie to social skills to musical or artistic talent to relationships with mom or dad. A girl can come to school in the morning totally bummed, and, by lunch, be hugging and giggling with her friends.

And then, of course, there are the physical changes. Nor is it simply a matter of height, weight, breast and hip development. The actual shape of the girls' faces change. When you look at the pictures of the students when they entered the School as 10-11 year-old 6th graders and compare their 8th grade graduation pictures just three years later, you can hardly believe it's the same person.

With every change, of course, there is growth. With every change, a middle-school girl is growing and developing what will become her adult self. What will become her way of seeing and understanding herself. What will become her way of living in this world. With every change, a middle school girl is shaping and molding how she thinks about herself and how she will think about herself for decades to come.

Change and growth are happening in every life, of course. Every day, we parents and teachers are changing on many levels in many ways consciously and subconsciously. But, in the lives of middle-school girls, the process is amplified, magnified and accelerated. A major life change that might take a year or two for an adult to grow into can happen to a middle-school girl in a matter of weeks or even days. And it is precisely because change is happening so fast in these young lives that it often becomes overwhelmingly confusing for the girl and utterly exasperating for the teacher or parent. What these emerging adults experience are nothing less than "growing pains." Not just physical growing pains, but growing pains in multiple areas of her life.

Over the years of operating Hanger Hall School, we have identified seven major areas of change and growth. Keep in mind that change in one area inevitably overlaps with another. But, in observing many middle school girls from many backgrounds, cultures and religions, these are some changes you might come to expect:

1. Psychological (Discovering, Exploring and Developing the Essence.)
The word, "psychology" comes from the Greek, psyche, which means "soul" or "essence." When we talk about a child's psychological development, we are speaking of the development of the soul. Development of the essence of the child. We may call it, "personality" or "character;" but when we become aware that during these middle school years, a child is actually growing her essence… growing her soul… the importance of this time cannot be overestimated.

2. Physical (Girl-Child to Young-Woman Bodies)

Some of it is obvious, of course: the height, the breasts, the hips, the hair, the menstruation. But during these middle-school years, every part of a girl's body is changing. From the size and shape of her feet to the color of and oils in her hair. From the way different foods taste to the way her body digests and absorbs that food. Metabolism shifts. Glands kick in. Skin tone alters. Muscles strengthen or go slack. The girl-body is fast morphing into an all-new adult-body

3. Emotional (Hormones & Apron Strings)

"The Moody Mountains of Middle-School," some have called it. Call it what you will, you can't ignore the highs and the lows - the peaks and the valleys - of middle-school girls' moods. Extreme-bouncing-off-the-walls-giggly-squealing-yelping-howling-like-chihuahuas-on-expresso to end-of-the-world-futile-hopelessness-with-crocodile-tears-wails-moans-and-abject –despair, the emotional climate of a middle-school classroom can change more quickly than teens can text the location of a big party. It has to do with hormones, of course. It has to do with sexual awakening. And it has to do with *the need to break away from home* doing battle with *the need for loving care and attention.*

4. Social (Connections, Connections, Connections)

Middle school girls love connection with other middle school girls. All kinds of connections: talking, laughing, dressing up, doing each other's hair, giving each other make-overs, holding hands, sitting in laps, snuggling in bed, texting, Emailing, IM'ing. Middle school girls love sleep-overs, playing soccer, talking about boys, going shopping, inside jokes, acting out musicals, jumping on trampolines… almost any activity, as long as it's with other middle-school girls. It is this extreme and natural social interaction which points ever so clearly to the advantage of single-gender schools and experiences. Likewise, these middle-school years are the most vital time for learning to be comfortable in talking with adults.

5. Mental (Ideas, Information & Opinions)
Curiosity may have killed the cat, but never a middle-school girl. Curiosity is the name of the game. Girls this age want to know. They want explanations. They want to discover ways of discovering things about themselves and the world around them. They may not use the same sources for information as their parents; but they seek it, nonetheless - from friends, from books, from movies, from family. Often, they seek it within. Girls this age find their ideas and opinions shifting. Likewise, they find themselves gravitating to and holding on even more dearly of some opinions which didn't really matter that much just a year ago.

6. Spiritual (Wondering – Exploring the Non-Visible)
Up to middle-school age, a girl often accepts her family's religious or non-religious values. From 10-14, these same girls often challenge these values and traditions. Not only do they not believe in Santa Claus anymore, they may begin to doubt other non-visible or spiritual beliefs or notions. And, at the same time, they may begin to discover their own unique spiritual connections through music, nature, romantic stories and feelings or friendship with a girl whose ethnicity and beliefs differ from her own.

7. Individual (No Such Thing as Pigeon-holes for Anyone)
Most important thing: There's no perfect way to grow from child to young adult. Every girl finds her own path at her own speed. One of the biggest mistakes that teachers and parents make is trying to push or impose growth on a child. Trying to make a middle-school girl "grow up" is like trying to force a flower to open. There are late-bloomers and early bloomers. There are bloomers who open a little and then close up for awhile. There are bloomers who show a bit of color now and no color the next day. The move from girl-child to young-woman is as unique for each person as is their fingerprint.

AUTHOR INFORMATION

Howard Hanger, founder and minister of ritual of JUBILEE! Interfaith Community since 1989, graduated from Emory University, BA, MDiv, in Sociology & Anthropology. While at Emory, he studied under Dr. Margaret Mead, whom he claims, turned his life around. As a jazz pianist, he has traveled throughout the world with the U.S. State Department and performed with his band, teaching jazz in hundreds of elementary schools across the country. He is the Founder of Hanger Hall School, a middle school for girls, which he started in 1999 for his daughters, one of whom attends Harvard, the other, a distance runner for Appalachian State. He has produced 14 albums or music and is the author of *Drink Deeply With Delight* (Lobster Press).

Dr. Vicki Garlock earned her undergraduate psychology degree from Brown University and received a Ph.D. from the University of Alabama at Birmingham with dual specialties in neuroscience and cognitive development. She spent 11 years as a professor at Warren Wilson College, teaching a variety of courses related to human development, biopsychology, and learning/cognition. She has published on the early predictors of reading achievement, the use of service learning and technology in the college classroom, and the extension of the adolescent period into the college years. She lives in Asheville, North Carolina with her husband and two children.